Praise for *The ABC's of Spirituality in Business*

"Spirituality in business is like the oxygen we breathe in our lives. It is beyond our senses; invisible, yet always there... sustaining our very life form. Rosie, through this book, makes this 'invisible' life sustaining form 'visible' to us. Peppered with real situations, the book is a treat to read and the real kicker is that you will see a part of yourself in every chapter."

Himanshu Jhamb, President & Co-founder, Active Garage

"Dr. Rosie Kuhn has combined two topics; spirituality and business, which often appear to live in different worlds. Rather than indulge in theoretical ramblings, Rosie speaks in straightforward language that shows how spirituality principles can enliven one's work in the business world. This book speaks clearly and honestly, and I recommend it to you if you seek to find your own authentic way to thrive in the modern world of business."

Robert Schmitt, PhD, Dean of the College of Psychology and Humanistic Studies, Saybrook University, President Emeritus of the Institute of Transpersonal Psychology / Sofia University

"*The ABC's of Spirituality in Business* uses a unique way to collate simple yet powerful ideas, and frames the essence of what it means to bring spirituality to the workplace. Dr. Kuhn provides an easy to follow guide to living in faith. By exploring the impact of concepts like power, anxiety, mindfulness and inspiration, this book provides valuable guidance to young professionals and seasoned executives alike in being more human in the workplace."

Pushkar Ranade, Senior Director, Technology Development, Suvolta

"Dr. Rosie Kuhn has written a clear, simple and readable guide to one of the most important and complex issues in business today: how can one be a true leader and also remain true to one's spirit and authentic self? Using a very simple organization, Dr. Kuhn's book will help leaders answer everything from A to Z about how they can be whole, loving, and connected while also achieving performance and profit."

David L. Dotlich, PhD., Chairman, Pivot Leadership, Author of Why CEO's Fail; Head, Heart and Guts, and eight other best selling business books.

Dr. Rosie's *ABC's of Spirituality in Business* is one of those rare "must read" books. It is clear, to the point, and practical, and at the same time, it is inspiring and expanding. I only wish that this would be required reading in every college business class and MBA program offered anywhere and everywhere. It would be a gift to humanity if it became required reading for every high school student their senior year! I love the ABC approach. It assists in planting these wonderful teachings and guidelines more deeply into ones conscious awareness.

Joyah French, Transformational Mentor / Teacher and Creator of Inner Alchemy in Half Moon Bay, CA.

Rosie offers us an opportunity to see how businesses can have a higher purpose beyond profitability, and why qualities such as kindness and integrity bring long-term success on multiple levels.

Debbie Gisonni, President & CEO, Stillheart Institute, Author of The Goddess of Happiness

"I am impressed with this book's vast basis in knowledge, scientific inquisition, and its message. It is truly a great document, worthy of great respect and attention."

Kim Hayes, Co-founder of Groundwork Strategy and Design Works

There is a Zephyrus breeze around us, an evolution to the economy of 'spirit' and 'soul' based businesses, and *The ABC's of Spirituality in Business* offers us a primer on how to navigate these winds of change. Don't be caught in the swirls of wind alone; allow Dr. Rosie Kuhn to be your guide."

Blaze (Barbara) Lazarony, Certified Transformational Life & Business Coach, Workshop Leader, & Author

THE ABC'S

OF

SPIRITUALITY IN BUSINESS

BY

DR. ROSIE KUHN

Book Cover Typeface: Adobe Avenir, Berthhold Bodoni, Berthhold Bodoni Italic

Book text in Times New Roman, headers and sub-headers in Cambria

Cover Design by Maureen O'Neill: maureen-oneill@comcast.net

Editing by Kim Harris: Strategicopywriter@gmail.com

Photo of Dr. Rosie by Reid Mason at MasonPhotographics@gmail.com

Publisher: The Paradigm Shifts Publishing Company
Orcas Island, Washington
ISBN: 978-0-9835522-4-6

Dedication

I dedicate this book to all of my clients. It is only through your commitment to living into the fullest expression of you essential nature that I have become wise enough to travel alongside you on the road less traveled. Thank you for the honor of your company. It has been a privilege thus far.

Intro: Bringing Spirituality into the Business World

If I were you, perched on the edge of your seat, curious enough to open a book on the topic of spirituality and business, I'd be readying myself for — what, I'm not quite sure. I know I'd have a couple questions in mind. I'd be curious about the philosophy or beliefs of this writer. I'd also be curious about what this topic has to do with me personally. I'd wonder if this is going to be some righteous, higher than mighty individual who's going to preach some dogma about what's right and what's wrong in the corporate or business world. Is she going to tell me to meditate or pray before, during and after every meeting —or to read the bible, the torah or the Vedas? That's what I would be wondering if I were you.

Spirituality in Business

My particular beliefs and interpretations regarding spirituality and more specifically, spirituality in business emerged through my own personal experience of exploring the edges of my comfort zone, as well as through the empowerment of many individuals in organizations and businesses who felt the need for a thinking partner. As they began to bushwhack their paths in business, they found that by including a spiritual component into their work life, they easily managed to shift into greater effectiveness and fulfillment. With this shift came clarity of intention and greater ease in following through with commitments to their role, their partnership with co-workers and the organization as a whole. Being more fulfilled, they were less stressed, more relaxed and more creative.

My perspective on spirituality in business is pretty simple: Regardless of the context, be it personal or corporate, I define spirituality in the most foundational and pragmatic terms possible. Spirituality is living in faith — faith not as religion, but practicing trust; opening up to what you don't yet know, and perhaps letting go of what you are firmly attached to, for something that may be tenuous at best. To practice anything new takes faith. I say a leap of faith is the essential and most fundamental practice of spirituality. That's it!

For me, what's required to even consider the possibility of engaging in life from a spiritual perspective is the willingness to be curious about who you are and how you 'be' you. It's being willing to cultivate awareness by exploring how you make your choices. This practice of being curious leads to self-realization, which leads one along the continuum of enlightenment, one degree at a time. Another important aspect of spirituality is the practice of actualizing your Self. That is, taking actions in the direction of how you want to 'be' — maybe even who you want to be.

Practice

You can hear that I am emphasizing the concept of practice. By this I mean exercising and developing the muscles required to be curious, courageous and to cultivate awareness, and to put this newfound awareness into action. Both practices take faith and the implementation of our faith-leaping muscles.

Here's a good example:

Only one out of five people experiences fulfillment at work. What that means is that to some degree, most of us are unhappy and unfulfilled in our jobs! Is that a spiritual issue? You bet!

Let's say you are one of those unhappy workers. How does your unhappiness affect a) your relationship to the work you are doing; b) your relationships with your co-workers, managers, bosses and direct reports; and c) your relationship with yourself, your family and your friends? When you are unhappy, what's the quality of that experience? How do you be unhappy? Seriously!

Everyone's answers will be different, but more often than not, I hear the following: *I am withdrawn; withholding; shut down;*

unavailable; and numbed out. My creativity disappears; I eat more; exercise less; and I waste a lot of time at work. So what does that have to do with spirituality?

Here's another question: If you are one of the unsatisfied, what is the source of that unhappiness or that lack of satisfaction? What is it that creates that lack of fulfillment?

Again, each of us will have our own unique list of responses to this question, and what I hear quite often is: *I really don't care about my company's product or service; the company treats us like robots; This place has no soul; I'm here for the money and prestige, but I have no passion for what I'm doing; No one listens to my ideas; I'm not being challenged in the way I was promised; I'm afraid that if I leave I'll never have stability or security again; I can't make the kind of money I want doing what I'd really like to be doing, so I'm stuck.*

Being stuck, unhappy and unfulfilled actually are choices we make based on our wants and desires. Too often, we have competing desires, and through the practice of choice-making, we have to prioritize our desires. Listing our hierarchy of desires will give us a good picture of how we make our choices.

It doesn't matter if you are an individual, a small business or a large corporation; on an ongoing basis, you make choices in service to your hierarchy of desires. The questions are: Is your choice-making process currently working for you? And, if it's not working for you, would you consider seeing things differently, to achieve greater fulfillment?

You can say *No, I'm not willing to see it differently.* That's good to know. However, I may ask another question: what has you say no? What has you not willing to see it differently?

Faith

Our commitment to limiting ourselves to what we know maintains the status quo. Just the willingness to consider other possibilities takes faith. It causes change and disruptions. Most of us would like a change, but we don't want the disruption that accompanies it. For many of us, maintaining invulnerability is at the top of our priority list. Exploring, experimenting with, and expanding our comfort zones require a willingness to take risks, and to be vulnerable. All new beginnings require vulnerability and a leap of faith. You already know that — you've already taken many risks to be where you are, right now in this moment. You exercised muscles of faith to get you here. There's no reason you couldn't choose to exercise those muscles again, in service to fulfilling your desires.

Kindness and compassion are also elements of a spiritual practice. Moreover, kindness and compassion within the work environment is profitable. People are happier, more creative and more likely to stay longer with their current company. Great! With all of this being true, how does an individual, business or organization bring spirituality, or the practice of faith, kindness, and compassion, into the workplace?

Through the ABC's we will explore and experiment with some very essential aspects of being human *and* spiritual in the workplace. It's really easy to understand the value and importance of the concepts shared here — it's another thing to actualize them. Through simple consideration and practice, you may find yourself cultivating Self-Realization and Self-Actualization — at work!

A: Anxiety, Avoidance, Acknowledgement and Acceptance

Beginning any journey — whether spiritual, business or family-oriented — begins by simultaneously building and stepping onto the path. Laying down the foundation can be done in any number of ways. If you've researched business training programs, you know what I'm talking about. A paraphrase I found from the Chinese philosopher, Lau Tzu (604 BC — 531 BC) said: *Even the longest journey must begin where you stand.*

We find what we need when following the impulse to begin. It doesn't matter where you start or in what direction you go. Beginning is the most challenging and courageous aspect of the journey.

I've chosen to adventure with you on this journey of spirituality in business using the ABC's. My intention is that through the simplicity of the alphabet, combined with the elegance of concepts I consider essential to a spiritual practice, you will be inspired to accompany me on this fascinating spiritual journey.

A is for Anxiety: Anxiety is the most challenging "A" word. What is labeled most often as anxiety, a sensation in your body that can feel very uncomfortable, is essentially one of the primal responses to life as a human being. It keeps us from doing things we shouldn't do. It keeps us in the fold of what others expect of us. That anxious feeling arises when we think beyond the current moment to include what may be beyond our comfort zone. Anxiety can be a control-freak in our lives. It can become the master that we serve. No one likes feeling the qualities of being anxious, so we do whatever it takes to make them go away. The dilemma is that our desired results generally lie on the other side of the sensations we call anxiety.

Anxiety also rears its ugly head when we futurize who we will be and what we'll be presented with. With the current instability of our economic structure, it's easy to ask *What if...?* What follows then is *Will I be able to survive? How will I survive? What will become of me?* These questions trigger anxiety, which functions solely as a survival mechanism. You're pressed to solve the life-threatening problem that causes you to be anxious in the first place. When we let the future take care of itself, we can then focus our intention on being present to what best serves our highest good and our highest truth today. In this moment, we can find a peacefulness that is not yet present in the future.

A is for Avoidance: Avoidance of Restlessness, Irritability and Discontent (RID). Underlying the majority of our survival strategies — our addictions and habitual ways of being — is the commitment to avoid the sensations of anxiety, also experienced as restlessness, irritability and discontent (RID). Distinguishing the choices and processes we develop in order to avoid what we don't want to be, do or know, is a huge practice. Yes, there is a great deal that we don't want to know or think about, much less feel or sense in our bodies. However, the choice to avoid discomfort will create significant obstacles, blocking each of us from having what we say we want. Avoiding discomfort will significantly reduce our capacity to cultivate a spiritual practice of any sort.

A is for Acknowledgment: As you are reading these words you are cultivating awareness (another important A word) regarding some foundational practices of spirituality in business. As you begin to explore and discover underlying sensations and strategies developed to avoid these qualities of being, it's imperative to begin the practice of acknowledging yourself and these processes. In doing so, you are becoming self-realized, and you are more at choice about how to actualize yourself. Your choices are in service to your essential self, your essential truth and that which you want to manifest in the world.

Acknowledging yourself is one piece of this practice. The other is to acknowledge others for choices they make or ways of being that make a difference to you. In the modern work environment, too often people are treated only as a resource. Their work is void of the humanity that is the essence of being in all of us. Lack of acknowledgment of our human being-ness creates significant challenges within every aspect of life. However, because we spend so much of our time at work, lack of acknowledgment here creates depression, resistance, low morale, resentment and apathy, to name just a few. The practice of acknowledging people lets them know that they are seen and valued for everything they bring to the workplace. Everyone is nourished through acknowledgments, including the person giving the acknowledgment.

You might think this is a no-brainer, but notice how often you acknowledge people for who they are and how they are being. Notice too, all the times you hold back from acknowledging people. Notice what shows up inside you as you consider whether you'll say something that lets someone know they are truly seen. Watch your resistance to saying something nice and ask yourself what creates that resistance. Then do it anyway — just as a practice.

It's easy to love the loveable and to say nice things to people you like. Cultivating a spiritual perspective means practicing kindness to those who may rub you the wrong way. What stops you from acknowledging them? What do you gain by avoiding an opportunity to be kind?

This is not an easy path, nor is it comfortable, for it is wrought with uneasiness, tenderness, agony, grief, anger, anxiety and fear. It's all about you and only you as you begin to explore how you 'be' you.

Self-empowerment means becoming self-determined. We face emotions, thoughts, feelings and sensations that at some point in time we empowered to be bigger than us. Through cultivating awareness we begin to take back control and exercise muscles that support us in limiting the interference of debilitating thoughts, feelings and sensations. We gain the sense of power from the inside out because we are aligning with our own wisdom. This allows us to live in purpose and face our fears more effortlessly. It is all part of a spiritual practice.

A is for Acceptance: *Grant me the serenity to accept the things I cannot change, the courage to change the things I can, and the wisdom to know the difference.*

What are you accepting as impossible that you actually have the capacity to make possible? Where are you wanting to avoid the whole conversation of what's acceptable and what isn't, in service to avoiding the anxiety and all that it leads to? To truly bring spirituality into business we have to be committed enough to ask ourselves these challenging questions; accepting that this is foundational to our personal, professional and spiritual practice.

B: Business, Breakdowns and Breakthrough

Business, as a context, can look and act as if it's at the furthest possible reach from spirituality. When I began exploring a career in business coaching I was initially turned off by all of the thoughts, interpretations and judgments I'd been carrying regarding business. Eventually I realized that what's true about business is based on one's interpretation. Business is in the eye of the beholder. By shifting my interpretations I was able to allow a greater potentiality for change. Well, I'll go out on a limb here and say transformation.

Initially, what business meant to me was ruthless, unethical and immoral practices. It meant power-hungry individuals sucking the life-blood out of anyone and everything for profit. It meant status, money, dominance. It meant people don't matter except for what they can do, compensated with the lowest salary possible. Not a pretty picture.

Not every organization looked like this but my projections of the worst of the worst were thrusted upon all businesses, which quite often included government, religious and political organizations.

My original interpretation has shifted from: 'If it weren't for Big Businesses our world would be a much better place to live in,' to 'Big Businesses contribute in incredible ways to social causes and humanitarian efforts. They've created miraculous technologies and innovation, which contribute to a much better world.' Business is not bad; it's the practice of bad business that's challenging all of us today.

There's Beauty in the Breakdown

Things are not looking up for the world economy and for business in general. We, the people, are demanding more of our businesses, whether local, corporate or global. We're requiring them to be accountable for the practices that, on the one hand are literally killing us, while on the other hand, provide innovative technologies and monies that generate so much good on the planet. We value the good they do, and are no longer turning a blind eye to the bad. The old paradigm can no longer sustain the pressure, and to paraphrase Einstein, *we won't be able to fix our global dilemma with the same thinking that created it.*

Inevitably, there will be a breakdown, and it won't be pretty. Heck, we are in the breakdown now, with few brave souls competent enough to take us through this turbulent course

14

unfolding before us. (This is a great opportunity to crank up the anxiety — whoopee!)

Breakdowns are required in the process of all growth and development. Ask anyone who has lost their job, their health, their families, their business or livelihood. They will tell you that tremendous good and personal growth came out of it. They didn't ask for it, but inevitably were glad it came. These are brave individuals who willingly faced the dismantling of their reality, not knowing if a breakthrough would ever occur. They could only hope it would happen in their favor.

Breakdowns are messy, full of angst, agony, horror, loss, humiliation, anger and resentment — humanity's toughest 'be-withs.' A 'be-with' is something — an event, a circumstance or situation you can't control or change — that you can only 'be' with. A Big Fat Be-With occurs when facing what we've avoided, denied or distracted ourselves from far too long. There's nowhere to go and nowhere to hide. And, IT'S UNCOMFORTABLE!

Breakdowns allow for a release of what no longer serves us to be completed and finished. What follows is a void of activity, something that drives most of us humans bonkers. Much like winter, when things are dark, bleak and cold, we're powerless to make the weather or environment be different. We feel helpless and powerless, and often begin to lose hope. All we can do is take leaps of faith, which may mean just staying in this moment until the next moment arrives.

Bleakness is inevitable in any paradigm shift. Even thinking outside the box doesn't get us out far enough to gain the perspective we need. Sometimes, awareness alone of the Big Fat Be-With is enough, and again the F word — Faith — that this too shall pass.

One very interesting facet of the breakdown process is that blame begins to take center stage. Individuals take inventory for their part in the breakdown, whether personal or organizational. They begin to see how their personal choices impact the company, family or community. Blame is a fascinating strategy that serves our desire to avoid responsibility, condemnation, rejection and humiliation. *It's not my fault,* allows us to ignore and avoid our own accountability. Over time though, all of us will have to meet ourselves, take inventory and willingly acknowledge our responsibility for things being the way they are. Not one of us is without blame.

Breakthrough

I planted some wisteria seeds a couple of months ago. They've undergone a difficult transition. I did the best I could to give them an environment rich with nutrients, plenty of water and sunshine. I watch with anticipation for signs of a breakthrough. Little by little their essential nature to burst beyond the hard protection of the seed pod unfolds. Tiny little shoots show themselves. They have endured incredible hazards, not of their own choosing. We rejoice in the breakthrough!

For individuals and businesses curious about incorporating spirituality, this inevitable paradigm shift will require bravery to confront breakdowns of the familiar, to serve something greater — a greater good for all.

Each business or business practice has emerged because of a calling, a knowing, a vision, or a dream. Innovation comes out of these dark nights of the soul. Few of us are brave enough to follow our dreams and visions. Few of us are bold enough to 'be' a stand for what we believe in.

Being a stand, is a phrase used in personal and leadership forums. It means that who you 'be' and how you 'be' is in alignment with what you say is important to you. Though the phrasing sounds incorrect, it's important to understand that who and how you 'be' is at the core of every choice you make. It is at the core of every choice your organization makes.

The major dilemma facing every business is the lack of recognition of the humanity running the business. It's balancing the elements of the people and the bottom line. Are the individuals just a resource, treated as such in service to the product, service and investors? Or, are people valued for their humanity, for their gifts, their unique talents and perspectives.

How does an organization shift the balance? How do they allow a breakdown — in service to the breakthrough?

Those of us in support of healthier business models and business practices; what's our role? How do we empower people to empower themselves and others to facilitate this paradigm shift? It isn't a maybe; it isn't a perhaps. As the paradigm shifts, we ready ourselves for a global meltdown. Don't panic, for it will be an amazing opportunity of greatest magnitude in cultivating awareness and actualization of a more spiritual orientation to every aspect of life.

C: Commitment, Consciousness and Creativity

Rarely are we 100% committed to what we say we want.

I'm assuming that because you are reading this that to some degree you are committed to the concept of bringing spirituality into business. On a scale of 1-100, what is the degree to which you are committed? If you were 100% committed there would be nothing to stop you and you'd be fulfilled in having reached your desired outcome. However, generally speaking, there are underlying or conflicting commitments that create obstacles to attaining our stated desires.

These conflicting commitments align with our desire to remain invulnerable, and to avoid what we consider undesirable. In essence, we want to remain secure and stable within our comfort zones, while reaching out and expanding our lives. However, expansion requires a willingness to take risks and be vulnerable. The degree to which we are committed to our conflicting commitment is the degree to which we practice avoidance, distraction, procrastination and denial. These strategies keep us doing more of the same thing over and over, yet expecting different results. What occurs is a dilemma, the consequence of which is a feeling of being stuck, confused, doubtful and lost. The bottom line is that we are confounded by the dilemma within which we find ourselves.

Dilemma

I'm prematurely slipping in a D word here, because this is where life gets sticky. How one chooses to be with dilemmas will contribute to the inevitable outcome of your choosing.

When we distinguish what we are committed to from our conflicting commitment, we see that we are at a choice-point. On the one hand we want change; but on another we want to avoid the undesirable consequences that accompany change. Hence, we have a dilemma. How do we choose? How do we respond to the either/or question?

Most of us are unaware of the choice-making process that has brought about this dilemma. Because of this, we compromise our stand for what we say we want, at the same time compromising our stand for what we don't want. We become professional fence-sitters. If you are interested in creating transformation or a paradigm shift within yourself or your organization, it won't happen by using compromise as a strategy.

What becomes clear as you sit with this dilemma, or choice-point, perhaps with a thinking partner who can see the bigger picture for you, is a couple of things:

First, either choice will require surrendering or relinquishing your attachment to the outcome.

Second, the consequence of either choice will mean being confronted by vulnerability and loss of whatever you are attempting to hold onto. This is the nature of cultivating spiritual practices within the workplace. It is an allowing of the unfolding of the natural course of things to occur in service to what you say you want. This is also when the practice of faith kicks in, as you begin to consider the possibility of crossing the threshold, anticipating that first step in order to begin this journey.

What's at Stake?

What I like about working in corporations is that there is far more at stake for individuals, departments and the organization itself, to actually walk its talk. The risk is greater and so is the reward. Not unlike any other institution and group of individuals, there is a culture and that culture has rules; some are spoken and some are not. Always we are walking the line between cultivating an environment that supports us and one that protects us. Again, if we are looking for a paradigm shift we have to surrender our attachment to this walking-on-a-fence approach to change and really challenge ourselves to practice acting in alignment with our speaking. What's at stake will be different for each individual and organization. Generally though, we are afraid of losing what we have.

The distinction between generic business coaching and transformational business coaching is that transformational coaching requires you to step into your commitments; to expand your comfort zone; to confront beliefs, interpretations, expectations and assumptions that may not serve you or your organization. You must create a practice within which you exercise muscles that cultivate consciousness and compassion for yourself and all beings impacted by the current paradigm shift. Transformational coaching requires you to be with the BIG-FAT-'BE-WITHS' that challenge current interpretations regarding personal gain and loss, as well as death of a way of being that no longer serves the highest good of all. It also requires a different way of choice-making in support of your commitment.

To choose to shift your commitment by even one degree is enough to allow movement towards your desired outcome. It's enough to empower you to be with the anxiety and discomfort that comes with letting go and letting your higher wisdom provide support; the consequence being that the process unfolds effortlessly. This is where the spiritual rubber meets the three dimensional world.

If Nothing Else, Cultivate Consciousness

If nothing else, cultivating awareness through the practice of noticing will inevitably create profound shifts. Consciousness generates a greater capacity to change, create and live from an empowered stand. This stand is grounded in a conviction to follow through with intent. It is far more powerful than just wishing and hoping for change to occur.

A fascinating phenomenon that is challenging to grasp from a logical/rational perspective, is that the process of intentionally increasing your awareness of what you want, and bringing yourself into alignment with that intention, creates a vibrational modification in yourself and your environment. This in itself generates profound shifts beyond your wildest imagination. What isn't in alignment with that vibrational state will either shift or will disappear. Transformation at its finest!

Consciousness results in self-realization that will inevitably translate into self-actualization. Failing to act in alignment with our realization — well, all things will remain the same except for the fact that we know more then we used to. As I said above, if you shift how you are being to align with your highest knowing, this in itself is transformational. You don't have to overtly attempt to change your world or your organization. Just notice, shift and allow. This in itself is bringing spirituality into business.

23

D: Dignity, Denial and Detachment

Whether employed, self-employed, unemployed or retired, we all inevitably support or are supported by a variety of businesses and organizations. In our interactions with these organizations, we want primarily to experience a quality of dignity. This means being treated as a sovereign individual of value, worthy of respect.

Disheartened by too many disappointments, we choose to cloak ourselves in various armoring styles. Through this strategy we attempt to mitigate the experience of being disempowered, which is triggered by attitudes and environments that are less than safe. We stop communicating authentically, with curiosity and interest, and begin communicating from *What does she want from me?* and *What's in it for me?*

Consequences of stressful conversations and work environments are such that each of us actually empower ourselves to choose ways of being that are disempowering. We choose to lower our heads, withdraw and withhold, generate far less creativity, innovation, and engaged sharing — often precipitating depression and further demoralizing environments.

We are all affected by our own unique ways of empowering ourselves to disempower ourselves. That sounds confusing but is nonetheless accurate. We want to blame others and remain unconscious as to how we are creating our own demise.

D.E.N.I.A.L (Don't Even Know I Am Lying)

Certainly we are affected by other people's attitudes, moods and actions. At the same time, it's important to get that they are also very much affected by ours. Our tendency is to want others to change so we can feel safe enough to change also.

Quite often people are angered by my suggestion that we are not victims to our circumstance, and that somehow we are collaborators and responsible for the abuse that is perpetrated upon us. My job is to provide an environment where people can feel safe enough to begin exploring possibilities by the examination of the role they play within any unsafe environment.

Distinguishing what it is you are committed to will facilitate a conversation that generates either a discovery process or a disempowering process. This is in alignment with our previous discussion regarding commitments and conflicting or underlying commitments. Disclosing both reveals patterns and processes that we are unlikely aware of, yet which present powerful and devastating outcomes.

Dilemmas

We want change in our work environment, yet at the same time, we are fearful of the consequences. This creates a dilemma and precipitates a critical choice-point in just about every arena of our lives, not just in the workplace. Again, getting clear about what you want and the degree to which you are committed can allow you begin to detach yourself from the debilitating perspectives and interpretations by which you have been living, being and acting. Through detachment, you create a more expanded capacity to witness how your choices align with your commitment. You begin to distinguish your actions from your thoughts, and then with intention, make choices that align with what you want.

Detach from Fear

Many individuals experience disappointment, depression and dejection in their workplace. It is clear they need to become their own advocate; not just by standing up for themselves, but by noticing how they may be contributing to their workplace demise.

A woman once asked me — *What are some things I can practice before going into a meeting where I feel 'less than'?* I encouraged her to first sit quietly and get clear with her intentions. What was it she really wanted from the conversation? Second, I suggested she imagine feeling the quality of that experience. This would allow her to embody her intention, and she'd be more likely to follow through. She reported back to me the following week that she used this practice and experienced positive results. She'd followed through because she was able to stay in the embodied experience, and remain in alignment with her intention.

Again, we have to be willing to detach from thoughts that precipitate sensations of anxiety and other discomforts. Habitually we act from these bodily sensations, so it's important to distinguish when we act from fearful thoughts, and when we act from our highest intention. We know it in our bodies.

Domain of Humanity

I want to be clear with you that we make our choices based on the ground of being that we stand upon; the precepts of which are either fear-based or essence-based. These precepts reside in what I call our Domain of Humanity.

Utilizing our personal power, we choose from either fear or fearlessness. Our current paradigm is fraught with fear-based realities that we presume to be true. Can we detach ourselves from those fear-based thoughts enough to allow possibility to reveal itself? Can we allow ourselves to expand our comfort zone to include what has yet to be conceived as real in our own thinking?

A fundamental practice that empowers this exploration is to distinguish the roots of your choice-making within the Domain of Humanity. Just by noticing what is occurring in your body — those sometime very subtle tensions or releasing — you can reveal to yourself whether the current choice is founded on fear or on essential wisdom. Only through practice will you be able to reveal fascinating choice-making processes that empower you, in the long run, to self-generated dignity.

E: Essence, Engagement and Empowerment

My experience with life in any business environment is that these three words: empowerment, essence and engage, are the most powerful. They support and enhance personal and professional growth for both you and the business within which you are employed. The degree to which you are engaged with your work and your environment from an empowered perspective is the degree to which you will experience fulfillment and healthy dynamics within the workplace.

In my initial interviews with clients, regardless of their position, I ask: *What might people find out or decide about you that you don't want them to know?* In quick order, even top executives will share aspects of their humanity that they are afraid will be discovered. They'll say something like *I'm afraid people will find out that I'm a fraud, that I'm unworthy of my current position; that I don't know as much as people think I know; that I'm barely able to cope with the responsibilities I have; that I sometimes doubt my capacity to do my job effectively*. The list is endless as each of us has our own unique set of truths about ourselves that we want to keep secret. This particular set of truths has us believe that we are inadequate, incompetent and unworthy.

The next question I ask is: *What do you do so people don't find out that you are (in this case) a fraud, unworthy of your position and the responsibility that comes with it?*

The answers to this question reflect a set of survival strategies, which over time become unconscious mechanisms we call our personality or ego. As you can see, our ego is fueled by fear-based precepts that would have us believe we are flawed and must alter our behavior in order to avoid being found out. Being found out, for most of us, translates into rejection, humiliation or annihilation. It takes an incredible amount of effort for our ego's radar system to constantly be on the lookout for potential slips that could incur being found out.

Imagine the amount of attention and energy you put towards this protective process, which I call your survival mechanism. It's much like your computer that is set up with a virus detecting software. It has to be on alert 24/7. In the case of us humans, though, we are alert for not only what might be coming in, but more importantly for what we might be putting out.

In the business environment, too many of us are working and being from our egoic self. *What else is there*, you might ask?

Free of Ego

Imagine if you will, a moment in your life when you are not operating from your fear-based strategies. What's that like in your body? What's the quality of the experience you imagine yourself in? Sometimes it's challenging for people to remember such an experience, because it's rare for them to not be stressed, fearful and on alert. However, most people will eventually remember a time, or at least begin to sense what it might be like. When they do, they describe the qualities of being in that moment as light, relaxed, free, creative, playful, fearless, engaged, connecting, open, flexible, even powerful. This list too is endless as there are so many adjectives to describe this state of being without fear. We know this place; we just don't visit it often enough.

The next question I ask my client is: *What would shift in your relationship to your work and your work environment if you were to come from freedom, creativity, calm, . . . instead of stressed, overwhelmed, intimidated, . .?* The answers always astound the person answering. *I'd be more accessible to my direct reports, I'd be more engaged in their projects; I'd be less controlling and would delegate more easily; I'd be more fun to be around and I'd support people in being innovative. I*

33

wouldn't be so stressed; I'd also be more willing to leave the office earlier, spend more time with family, friends and myself.

Wow! So by imagining being in a state that is not fear-based, all sorts of possibilities show up that may have otherwise seemed impossible.

Once an individual is aware that they actually can choose differently how to be in their work environment, they then can begin to exercise muscles that will help them generate this newfound freedom, fun and flexibility.

The 4 Questions to Ask

You would think that once experience and revelation has occurred, people would actually empower themselves to choose to begin the process of shifting from fear-based choice-making to what I call essence-based choice-making. This brings us back to that essential dilemma of wanting what is desirable, while at the same time wanting to avoid what is undesirable. Again, four basic questions need to be asked:

1. What might people find out or decide about you that you don't want them to know?

2. What do you do in order to have them not find that out?

3. Imagine if you will, a moment in your life when you are not operating from your fear-based strategies. What's the quality of that experience?

4. What would shift if you were to be that now? What choices would you make and what actions would you take in alignment with those choices?

This line of questioning consistently brings the individual in direct alignment with their essence of being, and empowers them to engage in actions that will bring about the desired outcome.

I totally understand how terrifying it is to consider being in your essence, especially in the workplace. Rarely are we seen or acknowledged for our essence-self. However, we are not our survival strategies. Those change as our circumstances change. We are not our egos either. If that were true we would never experience those moments when we know ourselves to be beyond fear and limitations. But knowing this doesn't make it any less scary.

This brings me back to my original introduction when I defined spirituality as the practice of faith-leaping. It's important to exercise muscles that allow you to consider the possibility of shifting from the perspective that *life is scary*, to, as Helen Keller said, *life is a daring adventure or it is nothing*. Engaging with your life as a daring adventure requires thoughtful presence to what it is you've come here to do, and to be.

At some point, you will realize you don't have a choice but to begin to get those muscles in shape. It isn't a matter of *if*, it is a matter of *when* you'll empower yourself to engage in living into your essence of being and to live your life totally on purpose.

F: Fear

The current paradigm within which we are rooted is cultivated solely around fear-based thinking. 70% of our thoughts are precipitated from fear. Imagine that! How did we come to reside in such an environment, permeated by fear-based thoughts? Is there another way? Do we have a choice in the matter?

In the previous section, I distinguished essence-based thinking from fear-based thinking. We have a knowing, without a shadow of a doubt, that we are something far beyond the fear-based reality within which we are immersed. At the same time, there is a field or paradigm that corrupts this knowing, obscuring the brilliant and radiant beings that we are.

Throughout history, human beings who do not conform to cultural, political and religious dogma have suffered persecution. This fact reminds us that we are not immune to the horrible things that human beings can do to one another. We remember and imagine what it has been like to be subjected to such treatment. And, at the same time, we may be living in conformity, unconscious of fear's pervasiveness in our everyday life.

Notice Your Thoughts

Imagine heading to work. You in your car, on the train or bus, and you're sensing some anxiety, resistance or something that isn't peaceful. If you were to just notice, for a moment, the thoughts running through your mind that catalyze these feelings, what would you observe? If 70% of what you think is negative and fear-based, what environment are you creating inside your head as you prepare to engage with work, others and your environment? Are these thoughts and bodily sensations preparing you for a day of peaceful, fun and creative interactions, or are they preparing you to do battle with yourself and everything that confronts you? Are they memories of what occurred in your past? Are they worries about what may unfold, or are you thinking about what you would like to say to someone who is really bugging you?

So much of what is occurring in our brains is random firings of impulses that have become habitual in nature. Honestly, we have no clue as to how many of these 'programs' are running concurrently in our brain. Some of them are essential and some of them are just a form of mental masturbation, stimulating endorphins and adrenaline that make us feel good about ourselves, while distracting us from feeling bad about ourselves.

38

Say STOP!

As long as we are in this game of focusing on maintaining what we've gained, avoiding loss of any sort, and ignoring the choice-making process, we will never fulfill our true potential. It isn't even a possibility because we've limited our capacity to think beyond the fear-based paradigm.

Einstein's words come to mind: *We can't solve problems with the same thinking that created them.*

There's a practice I've been working with for years. When I catch myself thinking fear-based, negative thoughts that do not serve my essence-self, I just say STOP! A couple of curious things showed up when I first started this practice. First, my fearful self wanted to review all the "what if's", "shoulda's" and "coulda's." And, it didn't stop. It went right on blabbering. Much like an unruly child, my mind had learned it didn't need to respond to my demand that it stop. I had to become more insistent before it would even consider listening to me. And...

I realized too that when that unruly part of me stopped creating thoughts that contributed to, well, essentially nothing, what showed up was fear. I found myself fearful of not having fear-based thoughts! I experienced a great deal of fear when I insisted my mind take a break. I didn't know who I was when I stopped thinking. Powerful! Feels like it needs a bit more elaboration though. What happened? How did you get past this fear of no fears? How did you figure out who you were without

39

your thoughts? Maybe I'm just curious, but I would love to hear more about this here!

Questions to Ask Yourself

In the workplace, we are constantly bombarded with circumstances that require an incredible amount of attention.

Here are a few questions to ask yourself:

What's the degree of quality attention you are bringing, and is it in alignment with what you want for yourself and your business?

Is fear, anxiousness, antagonism or resistance the foundation from which you want your actions to come, when engaged with clients, coworkers and others?

What commitment underlies this 'come-from'?

For me, when I'm committed to staying in an old story of a helpless, powerless, victim, I'm feeling anxious, worried and disempowered. I have to ask myself frequently; *am I really committed to that story?* I then have to give myself an alternative way of being that I am committed to: empowered, engaged and empowering of others.

Yes, I too sit in the dilemma of what to choose — my fear-based commitments or my essence-based commitments. More effortlessly than ever before, I'm able to take action in alignment with my choice to grow myself and my work from my essence-based truth.

Shifting the Paradigm

Shifting our fear-based paradigm into an essence-based paradigm requires each of us to be willing to perceive our reality through new lenses that reflect the *positive* attributes of our reality, rather than the *negative*. This in itself would make an incredibly profound contribution to our work environment, not to mention our family, friends and the world at large.

Start by being curious about your thoughts and emotions. Notice that your emotions are just energy that is generated by your thoughts. Shift your thoughts and you will find that your emotional state will shift immediately. I know it sounds like a lot to ask, however, I believe you are ready to step into this journey.

G: Gain, Greed and Generosity

Every organization, whether for-profit or non-profit, is in its line of business in order to gain something. It's most likely stated in their vision statement. My vision statement, for example, is:

The fulfillment of the human spirit through the empowerment of every individual on the planet.

This vision requires an acquisition of fulfillment and personal empowerment.

Gain

Whether to gain access to clean water, political power, or one's capacity to lead effectively, we are all out to gain.

With the economic downturn, businesses are facing major dilemmas. On the one hand, the choice-makers face potential loss of everything they've gained. All too often, this drives them to act in ways they believe will protect them from loss. Fear drives them to act in haste, making choices that may not be in alignment with their original vision. People make interesting choices when they are afraid.

We like to think of ourselves as gainfully employed or engaged, yet few of us want to associate ourselves with words such as greed. However, we are often unconscious of the degree to which we withhold out of fear. We are in denial, and our greediness is often disguised.

On the other hand of the dilemma, there are those companies that look at their circumstances, not from a fear-based perspective, but from one that can benefit many during this time of adversity.

Less is More

Do you remember the story of Ebenezer Scrooge, in *A Christmas Carole*? Scrooge's greed wasn't limited to money. He was greedy with his heart. We find out why, as we're given the opportunity to witness specific events in his life that created devastating loneliness and heartbreak. Because of these events, he chose to withhold and to be miserly with his gains, which greatly impacted many people.

Like Scrooge, every one of us experiences some degree of loneliness and heartbreak. We experience the inevitability of abandonment, betrayal and rejection. And, much like Ebenezer, we bury the pain deep inside, distancing ourselves from that pain, as it wreaks havoc on the façade we've invented. This façade has us look and feel powerful and invulnerable, yet inevitably, we find that it limits our ability to fulfill our true potential.

Fear is an enormously powerful muscle that is exercised far too frequently; so much so that we are unconscious as to how much it impacts our business of doing business. Our fears limit the pleasures of relating, connecting and sharing ourselves and our talents in service to our vision. We forget that this is what inspired us in the first place.

When we start to shift our contexts away from fear and withholding, we discover generosity.

All of us — the entire Human Race — have the capacity to overcome the adversities of our pasts. Hiding our hearts in a scrooge-like fashion, though, is not the way to do it. Practicing generosity can be.

This muscle called generosity is always with us. It just hasn't had a whole lot of exercise.

Exercising this muscle generates the experience of abundance, openness and allowing, innovation and expansion. Scrooge found this place after his journey with the Ghosts of Christmas Past, Present, and Future. He came to see that he had nothing to lose and much to gain by discarding his lengthy practice of greed.

As the paradigm shifts, we are so much more capable of witnessing our attachments to our gains, our fear of losing, and of finding that through some playful curiosity, we can discover fearless new ways to gain.

Those committed to bringing spirituality into the workplace may feel like they have an uphill battle ahead of them; however, simple exercises now can generate the necessary strength, courage and wisdom to engage in what's to come. You will find the shift easy and effortless — trust me!

Just for one day, I want you to try something: Notice opportunities to share a smile. Notice who you are willing to share a smile with, and from whom you withhold a smile. That's it! That's the practice.

You're probably asking: "What's a smile got to do with generosity?" Good question. I could explain it to you, but it wouldn't be the same as having you experience what happens when you smile. Plus, this practice isn't about whether you smile more or less. It's about noticing when you choose to allow yourself to smile and when you choose to withhold a smile. It's about noticing how you are choosing to smile.

Notice too, what it feels like inside you, while you choose to smile or not smile. Do this without judging or assessing yourself. Our actions can be so automatic sometimes that we aren't even aware of the thoughts or feelings we're having underneath. This noticing just allows us to cultivate awareness.

How can we embody the generosity we so wish to experience?

I have the following three suggestions:

1. Smile more often, even when you are challenged by your circumstances;

2. Notice your desire to complain about anything and everything;

3. Notice if what you do inspires generosity of spirit in your own heart. If it doesn't, consider doing something else.

Know that each and every one of us comes into our work environment anticipating and hoping that we will experience generosity of spirit from those we engage with during the course of our day. Like Scrooge, many of us don't have the capacity to even share a smile. See if you can share compassion to those who have less capacity to be giving of their hearts. Your compassion may be the most generous gift of the day. You may gain far more from that activity than you ever imagined.

H: Hope and Hogwash

Many years ago, before I had any sense of spirituality, a Buddhist friend of mine shared that most of us are constantly immersed in thoughts that are driven by hopes and fears. Think about that for a moment ... my thoughts coalesce around either fear-based monologues or hopes for pleasure rather than pain. There is a lot of energy going into this practice, eh?

When I'm immersed in thoughts driven by hope or fear, I'm not open to simply being here, in this moment. I'm not allowing myself to engage with new opportunities and ideas. I'm not being with what is, I'm being with what was, or what could be. What energy is unavailable while consumed in these unending internal conversations?

Our current paradigm has us feel as though we are victims to our current circumstances. This is absolute HOGWASH!

If and when we are totally honest with ourselves, we discover how incredibly powerful we are to manifest limitations beyond our wildest dreams. Yes, you read that correctly. We brilliantly empower ourselves to disempower ourselves. Remaining within this current paradigm will forever require you to live within your hopes and fears and nothing more.

Abandoning Hope

Hope springs eternal and is so essential to our sense of well-being. On the other hand ….

I've found that when used as a strategy to avoid the truth of our current circumstances, hope interferes with possibility. Hoping is actually not a very empowering strategy. The strategy of hoping leaves the power in the hands of the Universe. As we hope that the will of God or our Higher Power is on our side, are we relinquishing power and courage to change the things we can? We have to look at our own relationship to hope if we plan to participate equally in co-creation with our higher truth. How am I being while I'm hoping? Am I hopeless, helpless and powerless while I'm hoping? Or, am I engaged with actions that will bring about a more likely and favorable outcome?

My friend and colleague Michael Sky died yesterday of cancer, here on Orcas Island. Not only was Michael a friend, but he was also a support person for me and my business.

Michael had been ill for some time, yet no matter what his circumstances, we never gave up hope that Michael would remain with us in physical form. It wasn't until he actually died, did our hope die too. It's a terrible thing to be with — the loss of hope. Promised miracles and magic that continually inspire us to live one day to the next, vanish. We are left with nothing and no thing to believe in. We struggle to understand why. There are no answers forthcoming.

I believe that to surrender hope takes us outside the domain of our humanity, back to the Source of all that is. For most of us, this moment of transcendence is far too uncomfortable. Our mind struggles to make sense in hopes of finding concrete rationalization for what cannot be understood, only accepted.

Sometimes abandoning hope is actually the miracle. It may be what is required in order to shift what is currently impossible to become possible.

Grant me the Serenity to accept the things I cannot change, the courage to change the things I can and the wisdom to know the difference.

Letting go of hope frees us to look at life and our circumstances differently. It is not easy to take this leap of faith. Opening of our hearts, flooding ourselves with innovation, surrendering attachments; the result of which is to soar beyond our limited thinking — isn't this what we all desire? Isn't this why organizations hire executive coaches and consultants to create think tanks, so as to produce results through simulated means? Yes, they work to a degree, yet too often, the facilitators of change prevent their participants from actually leaping the full measure, of which they have no comprehension. How does one steward an individual through a leap of faith?

I have no doubt that this is where spirituality in business will take our organizations. Corporations are desperate to discover ways to shift their business. Eventually they will reveal that the seat of every employee contains the wisdom and brilliance they are looking for. Let's hope that realization comes soon!

I: Inspiration, Intention and Integrity

By the time you've opened your little peepers in the morning, you've most likely set your intentions for the day. This happens automatically for most of us. There are the normal patterns that we engage in to prepare for the day ahead, then follow through until tucked back in bed for a good night's rest. What would shift if we became consciously intentional about creating our day? What would we intend to happen? How would we intend to be that would allow our day to unfold exactly as we'd like it to be?

People can make extraordinary leaps of faith, creating because they were inspired to do so. Inspiration leads to intentions, which leads to acting with integrity. All three are essential, yet it is integrity that gets the job done.

You are a rare individual who considers the possibility of creating a paradigm shift in the work place; one that would allow kindness, compassion and true collaboration to inundate the ranks of the stressed, overwhelmed and unfulfilled. What arouses such an undertaking in you? In my mind it has to involve inspiration.

We all know what it feels like to be inspired. We spend thousands of dollars for motivational speakers to come and inspire us to — to do what? We read books and watch movies that facilitate the experience of feeling inspired. Too often, that inspiration doesn't last more than a couple of hours, and we are back to our normal routine. We know the experience, we know how to cultivate it— it's what we say we want, yet we don't make it happen.

Our physical response to the world is the tell-all of our reality. If you want to know what's true for you, go to the source—your body—it never lies. What does inspiration feel like to you? What causes that experience to move you to action? We don't think much about this, though it is a huge factor in our lives.

For me, inspiration starts with a sensation of giddiness and excitement in my chest. I feel exhilarated and want to do something to support and nourish this feeling of being swept up. It's different than anxiousness, which generally comes with a good dose of fear. I also feel an impulse to move, to do something that fulfills these sensations. It's like I'm being asked for something I know I can fulfill.

How does an idea manifest? Action has to be taken and initially this can feel energizing and fun. Slowly though, we lose touch with our original inspiration. With time and distractions, we forget what we wanted or why we wanted it in the first place. As we move towards what we want, a part of us may feel threatened, and that stops us in our tracks.

At this point, we need more than inspiration — we need integrity. Integrity is also a quality of being and we know what it feels like when it is present. Integrity tells us that in order to manifest our vision and preserve our well-being, we need to follow through to the very end. This all happens within our bodies. These bodily sensations continually influence us, yet rarely do we pay them the attention they deserve.

The Road to Hell is Paved with Good Intentions

The experience of intention can be very uncomfortable for people. For some, anxiety, nervousness and vulnerability ride shotgun. For others, excitement, anticipation and expectancy are present. What creates these different responses to the experience of intention? The vulnerability of wanting is embedded in our bodies, as are the memories of disappointment. The level of significance we give to what we want influences our willingness to set intentions to make it happen. More people than you can imagine have given up. They decided long ago that it wasn't safe to want, and most likely they weren't going to get what they wanted anyway. They wake up in the morning, yet remain asleep to their heart's desire.

The practice of setting intentions to create action and then follow through, while at the same time not being attached to the outcome, is essential and challenging. Living in the moment and practicing these steps strengthens character and gives us the courage to live into the unknown. It cultivates wisdom and confidence to be with whatever shows up. This too seems very challenging at first. But like everything else, practice allows us to be with what used to feel uncomfortable, vulnerable and impossible. Either it is enough to take us over the edge of our hopes and fears, into the life we imagine, or it's not. The only way to do this is by investigating this territory. We have to take the leap.

Inspiration, Intention and Integrity as Tools

On all levels of being, from our current circumstances to the domain of Universal Oneness, we have specific intentions. Without them we would not survive, for we would lack even the desire to hope or want life itself. To see inspiration, intention and integrity as tools, we can effectively change our relationship to that which generates the unfolding of life itself. As the paradigm shifts, each of us willingly participates in the expansion of consciousness, thrilled to witness the fulfillment of potential far more magnificent than imaginable. It is definitely worth the price of admission.

J: Judgment

Probably our single most damaging undertaking is the practice of judging ourselves. We judge ourselves, we project how others might judge us, and we judge others in relation to our own self-judgments. You can imagine how much energy this takes while moving throughout our day.

In the previous chapter, I shared that you have set intentions about how your day will unfold before you've even opened your eyes. That's because you have set judgments about yourself, life, your job, money— everything and anything. These judgments take the form of assessments, assumptions, expectations, beliefs and interpretations. Before your feet hit the floor you are operating based on what you've already decided will happen that day, and how it influences the rest of your life.

In your work environment, suspending judgment begins by flexing muscles that cultivate conscious choice-making regarding who you 'be' and how you 'be' in whatever role you play.

Chuck, a client of mine, works in the marketing department of a Fortune 100 company. At 47 years of age, he's at a point in his career where he is rethinking his plans for the next 20 years. Should he stay in corporate work and move up into a director position; leave Los Angeles and move back East to be closer to his aging parents; or should he go into a field that he is passionate about? He wanted a coaching session with me in hopes that I could help him figure it out.

Chuck does a good deal of comparing, especially how he measures up to others around him. He begins to think he should be more like Candice, who is strategic, smart, innovative and gregarious. He begins to slump in his chair as he describes her attributes. In many ways, Chuck is very accomplished and has had an exceptional life; however, he continually carries an extraordinary list around in his head of what and how he should be. He has little idea of what he really wants for himself because every one of his wants is followed by a "Yes, but, I should be …"

Within our session, Chuck began to observe the degree to which he automatically assesses his actions by projecting an assumed reaction onto his colleagues. He doesn't really know what their judgments are, but his thinking that he knows influences him nonetheless. He's judging himself based on preconceived interpretations about how he thinks he measures up or should measure up. This is exhausting. And, Chuck is not alone. Many of us continually assess and judge ourselves and others, and we have little idea that we are doing it. We don't allow a real authentic exchange of ideas to occur because we've practiced shielding engagements, which we believe protect us. We've already done the harmful deed just by assuming we know what we assume to know.

Change in business begins with you. It starts with cultivating awareness about how you 'be' and by noticing your judgments about yourself and others, be it your boss, direct reports, customers, or clients. It begins with acknowledging this automatic response and then getting curious about where those judgments and interpretations come from. That curiosity will begin to allow you to expand your awareness and to wonder how you came to choose what has become so automatic.

What's the Alternative to Judging?
We will always judge, compare, assess and interpret. These are essential and valuable tools in distinguishing and discerning what works for us and what doesn't. However, because they are used primarily unconsciously, they create more harm than healing. We don't have to stop judging, but it may be helpful to suspend it long enough to notice the value that judging brings.

If you want to bring change into the workplace, or if you just want to cultivate awareness in yourself, what is it that you want to practice in relation to judging, expecting, interpreting and assuming?

Notice when you judge something as right, wrong, good or bad. Notice where you judge something or someone as too slow, too fast, not enough or too much and needs to change. This also goes for noting these thoughts about yourself. The object of this practice is just to notice. And ask yourself: What's the point of this judgment?

What does judging and assessing as a practice do for you? How does this empower you? Does it allow you to create a change you desire? Does it allow you to feel righteous and better than, and if so, how does this impact the reality you want to create for yourself?

Coming back to Chuck for a moment: Chuck recognized that he was afraid of being judged. Through his continuous judgment of his work environment, he always played it safe, staying within boundaries he assessed as appropriate. Up until our session, he hadn't realized that this practice of judging and assessing is what kept him from getting promoted to a more senior position, where he would have to be innovative and take risks. He is now at a choice-point where he can consciously choose what he wants and what he is willing to practice to support that outcome.

The automatic thinking that we do always consists of judgments. Just bringing awareness to our judgments allows us to be curious about how true they really are. This allows us to choose differently, if it serves us to do so.

K: Kindness

Can a business create profitability based on kindness? Sure, why not?

The Dali Lama says if nothing else practice kindness. This must be a very powerful practice, so just what does it entail?

I googled the word kindness and here are a few words that showed up as synonyms: Accommodation, benevolence, compassion, courtesy, forgiveness, friendliness, generosity, gentleness, goodness, goodwill, grace, graciousness, helpfulness, humanity, perceptiveness, sensibility, sensitivity, service, tolerance, understanding and warmth. Who wouldn't want to be part of an organization that practiced kindness? Each one of these words embodies heartfulness: a quality of being mindful of the wholeness of the organization and its members. Each organization has a heart, just as each individual has heart. We forget this fact. We forget our own heart too. An act of kindness reminds us to be mindful of the essential nature of life that beats within us all.

In my google search, the words that came up as antonyms for kindness were: complaisance, compliance, deference, obligingness. These words reflected a different quality — not one that generates heartfulness. To me they reflect a stand for doing the minimum of what's required by the organization. They reflect an attitude of resistance to participate or engage. *I'm not committed enough to shift my stand or position. I don't want to and you can't make me.* What underlies this stand for complaisance and compliance?

Every one of us in a business environment is there for personal gain, first and foremost. Only as a secondary intention are we there to fulfill the vision and mission of the organization itself. If it were any other way we would set aside our judgments and interpretations, our fears and needs, our resistance and other survival strategies for the best interest of everyone in the organization. We would act in alignment with the highest good and the highest truth of ourselves, which is always in alignment with the highest good of everyone and, believe it or not, every organization. The fact is that we just aren't that committed.

Though we say we are committed to serving our organization, generally we aren't committed enough to shift our personal perspective in order to move beyond compliance and complaisance. What are we committed to?

I suspect many of us have a hit list — those people at work who we wish would disappear, with whom we avoid eye contact and conversation. It may be those about whom we gossip or complain. We may even perform passive-aggressive or passive-resistant maneuvers in order to sabotage their success or fulfillment. I'm always curious about what we gain from other people's demise.

Taking on a practice of kindness, just as a practice, will reveal underlying motives. Bubbles of emotions begin to surface that often feel uncomfortable. It's not uncommon for even anger, frustration and sadness to arise while practicing kindness. Attached to each of these emotions is a thought that is harbored in the recesses of your mind; a belief, a judgment, or interpretation that is confronted by just the smallest act of kindness. Though it is often uncomfortable, I encourage the exploration of what's interfering with kindness, compassion, generosity, graciousness. What do you have to lose? Funny, isn't it, that we think we have something to lose by being kind.

Kindness makes good economic sense. Good business and profitability comes down to creating good relationships. Good relationships require so many of the words above that relate to kindness. How are you practicing kindness or how are you 'being' kindness? Too often practicing kindness is a transparent, inauthentic manipulation, and personal gain is its motive.

Authentic Kindness — What's the Motive?

My work as a coach is grounded in authentic, engaged connection. When I am grounded in this I enjoy being myself and quite often find more to enjoy in the other person. I suspend judgment about who they are, their status, what I can gain from the relationship and remain in the moment, authentically engaged and connected.

Kindness, like compassion, is sometimes really challenging to practice; however, when doing so we can make a huge difference in our own capacity to be relaxed, open, free of stress and pressures. It contributes to our level of happiness and enjoyment. There is nothing to lose and everything to gain by just being kind. It's funny how such a seemingly simple practice works that way.

L: Loneliness

You probably thought that since we are talking about spirituality in business that love would be the L word. No. Everything we've discussed and much of what we will discuss engages and exercises the muscles of love. No need to go there today.

Though we spend hours with our cohorts, colleagues, and team members, rarely do we engage in such a way that we feel heard and seen for who we are and for what we really bring to the office.

Loneliness is a spiritual crisis for every individual on this planet. It is isolation from ourselves, our highest truth and our highest good. Its self-abandonment and self-deprecation that shows itself by the company we keep and the companies we work for.

We can't blame anyone for this malady from which we all suffer and to which we all contribute. All we can do is to begin to cultivate the awareness that each of us can contribute to the resurrection of the Self through conscious and thoughtful connection with everyone at work.

It isn't hard to cultivate connection — we've been discussing it all along. It's just a matter of deciding what you are committed to. Heal others, and you heal yourself at the same time.

Time to Google

I was unsure how accurate I was regarding the degree to which loneliness permeates our corporate cultures. Not every company or corporation is afflicted with employees that suffer from loneliness.

I googled Loneliness in Business and found one website in particular that shared many views of loneliness and how sometimes the loneliness and isolation in the working environment leads to depression, illness, stress, lack of motivation and the belief that *nobody really cares!*

Emily White, author of *Lonely: Learning to Live with Solitude* has a blogsite on the subject. It is an open invitation for those who experience loneliness at work to write and share their experience. Here are a few comments that I found valuable:

I feel invisible at work more and more. I'm a manager and my job is to promote the great work my staff does, which they do, but I find myself feeling sad that the people in our organization don't come to me for questions and the like.

I used to work for a small advertising agency and in the beginning, I felt it would lead to more friendships, but it didn't. ... there were also the usual stresses of personality conflict and turf battles in the office. Plus, the ... already well-defined cliques ...

I work from home by myself and the isolation and loneliness can be overwhelming. I do have to go to meetings occasionally, and I meet people for lunch every week, but it isn't enough.

A Lack of Shared Values

I asked a friend of mine, Jen, about her experience of loneliness in the Silicon Valley corporate world. She expressed that she had a lot of friends at work but found they didn't share the same values. This gave her a sense of disconnection and isolation. As she spoke about it today, eight years after leaving her corporate job, she realized that she was unaware of the degree to which she felt disconnected from those with whom she spent the majority of her days. She didn't have the awareness or the language to even know her own feelings. Her lifestyle today fulfills her requirements for connection, which she says is so important to her.

Bringing awareness to the quality of life we live within ourselves and at work can only begin to break the barrier of

silence we've created. It means interfacing with vulnerability —
as is always the case when growing ones spiritual intelligence.

Residuals of childhood patterning too often are the foundations
for the choice-making process we use to manifest our social and
professional environments. Choosing to choose intentionally
regarding your life and work environment will contribute in
phenomenal ways to the actualization of our spiritual growth, as
well as …..something to the effect of healing the loneliness. The
question to ask is — What is it you want?

M: Money and Mindfulness

Money

Money is very much a spiritual issue. Some think that the pursuit of wealth couldn't possibly be a path to enlightenment or spiritual serenity. We never know what our path will look like, what's in store for us, or where our greatest learning opportunities lie — awaiting our arrival so they can ambush us when we least expect it.

It's not money per se, but our attitudes and actions in relation to money that harm us and others. Fear, not money, is the root of all evil. When we fear we don't have enough, who knows what antics our survival mechanism will concoct to give relief from the incessant anxiety of *"I NEED MORE!"*

It's okay to want money, to have money and to spend money. All businesses are designed to manufacture or produce goods and services in exchange for currency of one form or another. This is a very good thing. We need this interdependent relationship to thrive. It's when those "G" words come into play

71

— greed and gain — that a healthy dynamic can turn dysfunctional. This is when abuse of power rears its head, and resources such as people, animals and the Earth itself become taxed, stressed and depleted of life force. Work environments lose their soul, and so do those whose lives depend on those environments.

Mindfulness

The balance of wealth and power takes mindfulness. Mindfulness cultivates awareness of how our actions, thoughts and being impact the environment within which we live and work. It's obvious that Mother Nature is beginning to demonstrate her lack of appreciation for how she has been ignored, plundered and taken for granted. And, because we are all part of this living system, I believe that She's indicating that we as a species, and as individuals, need to be more mindful.

I heard the other day that the extraordinary natural disasters that are occurring on this planet are caused by the inner turmoil of every living system on earth. We need to think of our businesses, corporations, religious and financial institutions as living systems too. Lack of mindfulness in the world is our responsibility, because all of us participate in the exchange of goods and services. We want what we want, when we want it. We can't keep passing the buck onto those who appear to be in charge. We are all responsible, and the practice of mindfulness will make that clear.

The Personal is the Political

We have no idea the degree to which our personal power can transform the world. To mindfully engage at work with integrity and a compassionate heart will allow you to move mountains.

Stress, disease and illness are caused by a lack of mindfulness. Healing brings about wholeness and awareness of the power we can use to shift and change ourselves and our environments. Acting in my highest good is acting in the highest good of everyone.

Mindfulness requires the intention to be attentive to what you are committed to. Pay attention to how you 'be', to what you do, to your thoughts, feelings and body sensations. This simple act will assist in the fulfillment of that which you desire. There's nothing to give up. There's nothing to lose. And, the gain in this circumstance is self-empowerment, self-honoring and the honoring of the sacredness of all that surrounds you.

Mindfulness also keeps us in the moment, present to what is within. We learn to be attentive to the impulses that move us toward fear-based or essence-based choices. There is so much more going on than you can imagine. And, it is so accessible.

As I write, I realize that M also stands for meditation. I'm not one to sit cross-legged on a pillow staring at my navel. My form of meditation is practiced throughout the day, staying focused and mindful of the agreements I've made to myself and to others. I emphasize, again, the notion of practice as a way to gain mastery, letting go of the idea that perfection will ever be achieved

N: Noticing

Noticing is the most powerful tool for cultivating awareness and for bringing valuable spiritual concepts to the workplace. Most important though, is having the intention to notice, in order to become aware of whether you are noticing or not.

Notice, for a moment, what is occurring within your work environment. Notice the lighting, the sounds, the smells and what the space looks like. As you notice, what senses you are using to notice? Is it just your hearing, sight, smell and touch? What other senses are engaged through noticing? What's happening inside your body, what emotions or sensations are present in this moment? Notice sensations, such as hunger, fatigue, stress, anxiety, worry, playfulness, humor or enthusiasm. Notice where you are putting your attention. Are you avoiding, distracting or delaying? If so, what or who are you avoiding, distracting yourself from, or what specifically are you delaying. Notice too, what it takes to be you in this moment as you notice and bring awareness to your reality.

A Lot Going On!

There is a lot going on, isn't there? By bringing attention to your reality you are able to get clear about what you are creating. By gaining clarity you are then able to notice what choices you are making and the results and consequences that ensue. What's the quality of experience you are having in this moment? Is this the quality of being you want to have throughout your day?

Bringing spirituality to the work place is an inside job. It starts with noticing how you 'be' who you be, and then choosing this to be the reflection of the environment you wish to create. Ask yourself this question: Do I really want to be the change I wish to see? If so, what needs to shift within me? Then begin to notice how you are in alignment with what you wish to create. You can only change what you are conscious of, and you can only become conscious by cultivating awareness through noticing.

On a Similar Note

My sweetie and I were playing Backgammon the other night, which we do on a regular basis. This particular evening we noticed that when rolling the dice, there were a phenomenal number of doubles. The odds were against us for rolling as many doubles as we did. Something was being brought to our attention — we couldn't help but notice it! We played six games and all of them were filled with vast amounts of doubles.

After Backgammon we decided to play some cribbage. Again, we couldn't help but notice that our hands consistently held three of a kind; again, way beyond the odds of it happening. There was no logical or rational reasoning. We had to go outside our current paradigm to understand the phenomenon that was undeniable.

Our world is full of events like this and they are occurring far more often than ever before. We are being asked to look and to notice what was once inaccessible to us. The cultivation of consciousness comes when at first we least expect it. Now more than ever we have an opportunity to witness a paradigm shift right before our eyes, at work, at home — everywhere. There is no doubt that this phenomenon is world wide — Universe wide.

Each generation that has gone before us has facilitated a greater and greater degree of consciousness. Many of you have heard, I'm sure, that we are standing at the precipice of a grand paradigm shift. We are generating this shift and at the same time it is being foisted upon us by cosmic activity far beyond our wildest imagination.

There are two ways one can respond when considering this unfoldment of the Universe. We either allow ourselves to be scared out of our wits and bury our heads in the sand, or we watch the extraordinary evolution of our time with fascination and curiosity. Some call it the time of the apocalypse, when we will pay for the sins of our fathers and their fathers before them.

Some call it the end times, but perhaps it is something else — perhaps even the end of the concept of sin and fear and war and sickness.

If we take on a practice of noticing, we can begin to see opportunities to consciously participate in this shift. By cultivating awareness, we will bring about a different way of being human: shifting from a fear-based paradigm to one based on our essence of being — love, kindness, compassion and creativity. A way of being that inspires each of us to empower others to live into their fullest potential — no holds barred!

O: Obligation

One evening as I was laying in bed, preparing for a restful night of slumber, a voice inside my head shouted: "I want to live my own life!" I was shocked by this outburst as I am one of the most independent individuals I know. I live on a secluded island off the coast of Washington, and I work independently and live happily in my very solitary existence. What more is required for me to live my own life?

I realized later, that although I live and work alone, there are many people to whom I feel a lingering sense of obligation and responsibility. They live in my memory as unresolved disappointments that burden and exhaust me, and keep me from fully taking flight in the way that I imagine. They continually remind me of everything I should have done but didn't because, well, I took the road less traveled. What becomes clear is that until I resolve my relationship to my belief about obligations, I'll never truly live my own life.

All of us carry a tremendous burden with all sorts of obligations, and we don't even know it. Or, we carry them because we think we are obligated to. I mean, where would we be if each of us let go of this sense of obligation and responsibility? Think of all of the opportunities to say or do what is in your highest truth, but because of your sense of obligation, you deny yourself. And for the sake of … what?

The foundation of the work that I do as a transformational coach is to ask these very questions to my clients, giving them an opportunity to figure out to whom and to what they are truly interested in being obligated.

I grew up within the Catholic Religion. I learned early on how to live in a state of obligation. There was a great deal of guilt and shame. Until I was seventeen, when I left the Church, I was terrified I was doing it wrong. It didn't matter what it was, I was obligated to do it right, even though I might not know what right was — and right according to whom?

All religious institutions require obligations. Family, community, government— all organizations require some form and level of obligation. How we respond to these obligations generates the quality of life we live, as well as the stress and dis-ease that is so prevalent in our culture.

A couple of weeks ago, a friend of mine decided to visit Orcas for an undetermined amount of time. She felt compelled to travel 26 hours from Omaha in order to be on the Island for — well, she didn't know why — but she had to find out. She called to ask if she could land at my place for a few days and figure out what was next. I said sure, and looked forward to seeing her after many months apart.

A week into her visit, I found myself struggling with the fact that part of me was ready for her move on to what was next on her adventure. However, what I was hearing was how she wanted to make the cabin a little more convenient for herself so she wouldn't be such a bother. We were sliding into conversations that sounded like she'd be staying for the whole summer — maybe longer.

I love my friend but I love my solitude more. Yet I questioned my desire for my sanctuary to be free of guests. Was that *really* what I wanted? A part of me felt obligated and responsible to take care of my dear friend. After all, she'd come all this way, had no money left for rent, gas or food, and she needed a place to stay. Shouldn't I be willing to help her out? Isn't that was friends are for?

What was my obligation, really? I had agreed to just a couple of days. And this was her adventure — her journey. For me to feel obligated created resentment and a slow deterioration of our friendship. I could feel myself begin to withhold and withdraw. It was time to check in with myself and then with her.

My fears have kept me blind to my own truth, yet I was afraid what she might think or decide about me if I asked her to leave with empty pockets, gas tank and tummy. What kind of a friend would do that? I'll tell you, it wasn't easy, but I told her that she needed to continue on with her quest, seeing what else was in store for her. Fortunately, she's the kind of friend that understood completely and within a matter of days she found a source of income and a new place to stay. That's the way the Universe works!

As a professional business person, my work-life needs to reflect this clarity of integrity too. Where do my obligations interfere with being the most effective at my work? Where do I take on obligations that really aren't mine to begin with? When do I take responsibility for the consequence of other people's choice-making? When does my own choice-making, based on other people's problems, cause further challenges to my clients, work environment, and associates?

It takes a great deal of courage to ask yourself these questions, and even more courage to speak or act in alignment with your highest truth. Yet in order to bring spirituality into business we have to ask these hard questions and we have to follow through. When we act in our own highest good we are acting in everyone's highest good.

Stepping onto the path of self-realization is a fascinating journey. It means being open to answers that may initially feel uncomfortable, yet in the long run allow for a greater level of wisdom to emerge. This allows for self-actualization to occur easily and effortlessly.

Obligations are obstacles to being in alignment with our highest truth. This is a very different way of thinking but one that will lead to the paradigm shift.

P: Power

In my first book, *Self-Empowerment 101*, I devote the first chapter solely to the subject of power. The reason is that every event since the Big Bang is a result of power and the energy that generated it. Regardless of who uses power and how it's used, it all generates from the same source.

Power is often synonymous with force, against sentient or non-sentient beings, for the sole purpose of gain. Gain is a reward that spurs us to generate unreasonably creative uses of power. Some of it seems absolutely ridiculous, like the guy in Norway who used his power to devastate the morale of a whole country. His motive was to gain recognition for his disdain for the rights of people he hated.

Other people use their power to stay under the radar, thinking this gains them freedom to ignore certain responsibilities taken on by those above the radar. Using power to stay small also gains invisibility from potential harm. Too many of us use our power to gain immunity from rejection, abandonment or betrayal. We may strive for invulnerability for the sake of avoiding the experience of losing control over the situation, other people and ourselves.

At the same time that we may use our power to gain what we interpret as control, safety and invulnerability, we also use it in the service of good and truth. Extraordinary creations make their way into our reality every day that make this world a better place to live. More and more people utilize their personal power to empower others. It's a beautiful thing to witness.

All of us want a sense of control in our lives and we engage our personal power to do whatever it takes to make that happen. We might use power to appear and feel disempowered, allowing ourselves to be victimized in ways that seem to be out of our own control, but really aren't. Yes, the individuals killed in Norway by this crazed individual were victims and they were totally vulnerable to the circumstance they found themselves in. It's important to distinguish when we use our power to create self-victimizing circumstances and when we are just plain out of control. Even in such circumstances we can still use our personal power to 'be-with' what is, in the best possible way. It may not save our own life or the lives of others, but we can at least step into a more empowering interpretation.

Power and Empowerment

For some reason I find the notion of empowerment far more helpful and available than talking about changing your use of power. It's essentially the same thing, but for me something changes with that one little *em*. Embodying, owning, self-governing, self-referencing, choosing to infuse oneself with the ability to self-regulate based on the outcome you want — that's empowering.

Ben, a client I'm working with in Israel, is the owner of his own successful business. He rules based on control and domination. He uses his power to disempower others so he feels more in control. Ben is always looking for reasons to make others wrong so he can feel righteous. By feeling righteous he feels in control and powerful. At the same time, his use of power doesn't allow him to have a sense of connection with his employees. This contributes to a sense of dissatisfaction in all parts of his life. He sees that his GM has a great relationship with the employees because he leads differently, and he's happier. What my client wants to gain from our coaching relationship is more fulfillment in his personal and professional life. He is beginning to understand that he experiences a greater sense of fulfillment when he allows himself to dismantle his current use of power. Ben is now willing to notice how he uses power in his business, and, he's finding that it means shifting how he uses power in his personal relationships as well.

What brought my client into coaching was that despite his power and success, he felt unfulfilled. He realizes that this is far more important than power and control. The invulnerability he gains from the way he's been using his power isn't satisfying. He's considering the alternatives and is cultivating awareness by noticing what's going on around him, how he impacts his environment and the professional and personal consequences. He's becoming fascinated with the mechanisms that influence the results showing up in his life and business.

Ben gets now that he doesn't have to give up one iota of power to have fulfillment. He gets that he can use his power to make different choices, maintaining the sense of personal power he had when he yelled at everyone. Nothing is taken away. However, his belief that people won't respect him if he doesn't yell will be tested. He is willing to experiment, because he has something at stake that is greater than his fear of being vulnerable and out of control. Fulfillment has become a big enough goal that he's willing to risk some pride — albeit, false-pride.

As the paradigm shifts, it becomes obvious that our business-as-usual mentality is causing incredible dis-ease in our work environments. Using power to maintain control in an environment where control itself disempowers the organization and its employees is crazy-making. As a culture, we are beginning to experience the requirement for less use of power

as a manipulative force, and more use of power to empower
others.

Q: Question Reality

Many years ago I saw a bumper sticker that read "Question Reality!" Up until that time my life had been a mish-mash of confusing circumstances, and it was a revelatory experience to take these two words into my soul. I breathed deeply and felt as though I'd been given a sign that there was light at the end of the tunnel.

At the same time, the context of my life did not include any mechanisms, supports or guidance that would allow me to question reality as an overt practice. My parents raised my siblings and me as Catholic. It was a sin to question anything or anyone regarding the authority or truth of what was to be believed.

My context as a female in Middle America also didn't allow me to ask questions that would potentially ruin my identity as a calm, submissive woman who could be wise but not too intelligent.

College gave me the opportunity to explore and witness realities lived by other people. However, I continued to interpret those realities based on what I still held as right, wrong, good and bad. At the same time, many professors also disallowed the questioning of the realities they presented.

Perhaps, all of these obstacles provided opportunities to *covertly* practice the art of questioning reality. The value of not being able to seek the wisdom of others to tell me what was real or true, was that I had to do the research and experiment on myself. Today, in the field of research design, this form of study is called heuristic investigation. Heuristic study refers to experience-based techniques for problem solving, learning, and discovery. This method of exploration and investigation includes using a hunch, an educated guess, an intuitive judgment, or just plain common sense.

What do you do when the world presents you with a reality that isn't connected to common sense? What most of us do is conform, distort and contort ourselves as best we can into the context of the reality that is in front of us. We rarely question or use educated guesses, intuitive judgment or common sense; or even look at the evidence in front of us.

As the paradigm shifts, we see the dissolving and dissolution of the foundation of our economic reality. We see the premier leaders of our financial, religious and government institutions fail to maintain systems that are literally bankrupt in their principles and practices. How do you make sense of that?

In the world of business — the buying and selling of goods and services — questioning reality means dismantling the whole kit and caboodle and re-inventing based on reality. But first you have to question reality!

There came a time when I chose to end the transformational coach training program. I had designed and facilitated this program for 10 years in Silicon Valley, California. My intuition had been guiding me toward this for years, but I was finally ready to make the leap. While discerning the common sense of this decision it seemed totally irrational and illogical. This program had been my bread and butter. I'd developed a reputation and people were flying in from all over the country to participate in this one-year training. What would possess me to give all of that up? Logic and reason were not the major players in this process, and I could do nothing else but question reality. Over the course of this past year, I questioned everything, and now, I hardly recognize the me that I've become. My anxiety is virtually gone; I'm far more calm and peaceful, I laugh far more often and the work I bring into the world is fulfilling. I love it! Questioning the reality I created over five decades offered me an opportunity to explore a reality far beyond the dogma of any religion I've ever known.

A House of Cards

It's becoming too obvious that there is a dismantling of reality as we've known it. And, you are required to play the game. You, me and everyone else in the Western World have built this house of cards we call our reality. Generations of individuals over hundreds of years have brought us to the last cards of the deck. It has culminated into this wonderful masterpiece. And now it's time to dismantle the house, either with deliberate consciousness or with a deliberate whack from the proverbial two-by-four. (Don't you love it when the cards go flying all over the place?)

What I want is for you to question how you 'be' in relation to the reality you call your life and your work. What intentions are being served by your current use of what you consider to be common sense? What flies in the face of this current reality that you hope will go away if you ignore it long enough?

I don't know if we'll be saving the planet. I don't know if we can change the foundations of the belief that we are safe from vulnerability. Earthquakes, real and metaphorically, have shaken reality as we've known it. Fractures, cracks, and fissures leave us dumbfounded with where to begin. Tsunamis, real and metaphorically have washed away the shelters, vehicles and the livelihoods we depended upon. What is the reality that exists once we realize that it's all gone?

Nothing Matters and What if it Did?

People with faith (not faith as in religion but faith as in people who put complete trust in a higher power) have something that is the true foundation of reality. I have no doubt they have questioned the reality in front of them. They've decided there is a reality that holds this one in the palm of its hands. They are able to hold the bigger picture and make choices based on this larger paradigm. These people usually share kindness, generosity and compassion effortlessly. Their values dictate choice-making based on spiritual principles instead of social and institutional mandates. They live in integrity and dignity and are accountable for their commitments. Some of these people are my clients and they are managers, CEO's and COO's of businesses and corporations around the world. I'm learning from them that to question "status quo" reality infuses the world with an innovative, higher-minded reality that, if nothing else, will allow them to empower others to fearlessly question their own reality. This is how every invention and revelation has come about. Why stop now?

R: Resistance

I'm experiencing resistance to writing this piece. I feel angry, frustrated and distracted by, well … It's more that I'm allowing myself to get distracted. That way I can avoid being with what I don't want to be with.

You might be asking — as I would if I were you — why the resistance, if I'm in the business of writing?

Even though I enjoy writing, it's challenging at times to articulate exactly what I want to say. In this moment, I'm trying to make sense of the idea that resistance is an important concept to include in a book on spirituality in business. I'm an intuitive writer; I just transcribe what's coming through me. I know that sounds a little whacked. However, I find that this way of writing is far more enjoyable, revealing and insightful. And, sometimes I have to deal with confusion, uncertainty, doubt, and, on occasion, feelings of inadequacy. I resist having to be with these feelings. I'd rather go do something easy and fun, where I don't feel vulnerable to the possibility of humiliating myself.

Often there are aspects of our work that we resist because we don't like being engaged in activities that challenge us. We get bugged by people, places or things and put the brakes on, dig in our heels, avoid, distract or ignore what's in front of us, in service to resistance. Resistance serves to avoid the discomfort of vulnerability.

Resistance at Work

My work in corporations brings me face to face with people resisting the very work they are paid to do. I'm stymied by the degree to which people resist the responsibility, collaboration, management and leadership they agreed to. People resist doing what they've come here to do. I find that fascinating!

For many, the rules of the game in any organization are unknown. You have to play your best poker face, your best everything, always — if you want to get ahead, get that raise, or earn coveted praise. You have to resist direct confrontation or insults; you might resist sexual innuendos. You have to resist getting fired and some people resist getting promoted, but they can't say that — it's not politically correct.

One manager I worked with in the Silicon Valley felt threatened by anyone who showed any inkling of being smarter than he was. He had many opportunities to empower his team members in ways that would enhance their performance. However, because of his belief that no one could outthink him, he resisted acknowledging and encouraging his direct reports. Many of them shared with me that they felt frustrated and limited in their capacity to perform. The morale of the whole team was diminished because this manager was afraid someone might outdo him.

This isn't uncommon — we all know that. Resistance runs rampant in every institution, enough so that we are resistant to calling this game to a halt. There is something at stake! That something is precious enough that we don't want to give it up. That something has a big price tag on it. Actually, it has two price tags on it. One is the sale price — the price for which you are selling your soul. This price tag reflects the selling of our integrity, truth, and fulfillment for the sake of power, position, control — and as always, the illusion of invulnerability. The other price tag, of course, is the cost of getting ahead, no matter what!

Resistance is an interesting set of muscles that we exercise in service to developing strength, control and power. It's also a survival mechanism we've developed over time. Quite often, like many of our survival mechanisms, it becomes automatic and unconscious. We're unaware of why we engaged those muscles in the first place. But a point I want to make here is that we have no idea how much energy it takes to resist. It's something you might want to think about.

Resistance looks different for everyone, but what's important is for you to discover, recognize and acknowledge your own particular style of resistance. Like I said, we are all doing it; it's just a matter of how and to what end.

As the Paradigm Shifts...

As the paradigm shifts we awaken slowly but surely to our own unique contributions to the way life is, as opposed to the way we desire it to be. We see where we resist shifting and changing as an attempt to hold on to what we think we've got, even when what we've got isn't necessarily what we want.

Sometimes the practice is to resist resisting; go with the flow, ride the tide! But first, we have to become aware of the fact that we are resisting, and what that resistance serves.

You may have heard me suggest this practice before, however, here it is again. It's the simplest practice: Be Kind! Kindness costs nothing, takes no time, and contributes greatly to peace on Earth. By practicing kindness, you will encounter your resistance to being kind. This is the moment we've been waiting for, where you can begin to question the value of resisting. You are at a choice-point where you can begin making choices differently. The opportunity to self-realize is upon you, and with that comes the opportunity to be the change you wish to see. Wha-hooo!

S: Sacrifice

I grew up in Michigan in a large Catholic Family in the 50's and 60's. I was taught that sacrifice was the price you paid to get into heaven. In service to this, I let go of my wants, needs, thoughts and feelings. What I was left with when I hit my 30's was pretty much an empty shell of a being, and I became, to some extent, robotic — looking exclusively outside of myself for commands to follow. I was terrified to think, feel or act on my own volition. Having never been given the How-To Manual for being me, I had no idea what course to steer to get to my true north. However, over the following decades, I taught myself how to listen to my internal wisdom, retracing my steps (from before I could even walk) to rediscover the fullest expression of myself.

In the name of Heaven we make incredible sacrifices. The question is — what is Heaven? More importantly in the context of this book, what is Heaven to you? How will you know when you've arrived?

Given that we are talking most specifically about spirituality in business, I suspect that each one of us has maneuvered into our current roles and positions because, to some degree, we want to create Heaven on Earth, especially when we spend at least one-third of our lives in this work environment. What have you sacrificed in order to be where you are right now, in this moment? What I really want to know is — have you sacrificed the *right* things in order to have what you currently have? Rarely do I use the word "right", so I'm obviously on the way to making a point!

A few months ago, I spoke to the San Francisco Professional Career Network. These individuals are in the process of returning to the workforce, however, many of them are up against some very stiff resistance (the R word, remember?). Not much different from many of us, they experienced rejection, trauma, abuse, neglect and humiliation in their previous work environment, and as they move in the direction of employment, something stops them. The obstacle they face is the memory of what they've sacrificed in the name of stability, status, and a sense of personal and professional fulfillment. This time, though, they have the opportunity to choose what to sacrifice, if anything, from a more conscious perspective.

Everyone has a choice to sacrifice and what to sacrifice: Health, family, personal fulfillment, creativity, integrity, financial stability, trauma, stress, abuse. Each of us has our price.

I'm suggesting that maybe what we've sacrificed isn't worth the price. This is a huge spiritual issue for those who believe that financial stability will create happiness. The current global economic circumstances indicate that this may be an inaccurate assumption. The wounding that has occurred for the sake of financial viability has cost many believers their lives, families, and dignity. I don't think this is working very well — do you?

I'm guessing that when you search your internal database, you'll uncover regrets and lost dreams that were sacrificed. At the time your choice seemed appropriate, or the only choice to be made. But for what? All of us have these regrets and losses, yet until we confront them and begin to mine the emotional well of powerlessness and hopelessness, we will continually repeat the cycle. We'll never allow our essential self to guide us to our fullest expression.

It makes sense to me that many of those individuals in the San Francisco Professional Career Network balk at returning to the corporate environment. I understand why they are no longer willing to sacrifice their souls for the almighty paycheck. It makes sense that many are ready to engage their passion, their courage, and their faith, with full thrusters on. Their trajectory: to discover the work that is theirs to do that's both fulfilling and meaningful.

Not all work environments are dysfunctional, but the fact of the matter is that too many are. My belief is that because most of us were raised in families where dysfunction defined us, how we came to see, value, and treat ourselves, we can't help but create environments that reflect the same.

I believe that each of us has come to this planet to fulfill a very specific life purpose. My job is to support people in choosing to live into that purpose — fearlessly. This conversation definitely includes the question *"What gets sacrificed?"* It also allows evidence to speak for itself; *"Has it worked so far to give up what is most essential to your BEING and to living your LIFE PURPOSE?"*

This line of questioning emphatically points to the dilemma, and what we do in response to the dilemma. The dilemma is a choice-point where most of us choose NOT to choose, thus experiencing a quality of life that feels stuck, lost, trapped, confused, and depressed. SIGH! No one gets the *"get out of jail free card,"* when facing the inevitable choice-point. Now or later — it's up to you!

I don't wish this moment on anyone; however, the inevitability of it is what it is. I can't convince or cajole you to take me seriously. I only encourage you to feel into your heart and soul and reveal, discover and acknowledge your own evidence, truth and wisdom to know what is yours to do.

T: Turbulence

To state the obvious, there's no question we are living in turbulent times. The winds of change are creating upheaval and instability, leaving chaos and confusion in the wake. The almighty dollar upon which we've built most of our institutions, including religion, as well as our sense of security and stability, is rocking and rolling like those areas around the planet that are experiencing earthquakes. Everything is getting shaken up.

In the workplace, job security is becoming a bankrupt concept. And, if you manage to keep your job, most likely you've taken on the work of those who have lost theirs. More stress and less fulfillment.

Naomi, a client of mine in San Francisco, used to love going to work every morning. Now, with a new CEO pressuring the very small staff to produce way beyond their capability, the strain is such that she experiences overwhelm, frustration and, what we normally call depression. "What's the point?" Naomi asks, rhetorically. "I used to love my work, but now I'm thinking of leaving. It's all too much!"

As a sailor who crossed the Atlantic Ocean, I could see the changes on the surface of the water that told us whether we're in for turbulent or calm seas. I could see miles off in the distance any sea change that was coming our way. I could prepare appropriately and, if need be, settle in for stormy weather.

Though I fly frequently, I am disconcerted by turbulence in the air because it is invisible, generally speaking. I look out the window intending to discover the catalyst for my discomfort. As an analogy, I find that these current economic and life instabilities we are experiencing are much the same. Where or what is the instigator of all of this turbulence in our institutions, our solar system, in the Universe at large? I find it fascinating!

The invisible catalyst is a known entity to those who see the larger spiritual perspective. However most of us feel victimized by the unseen forces that have wreaked havoc to our lifestyles, our sense of security and stability. We are losing our ground of being that we thought was us! Every aspect of life is getting a good shake up. I pose these questions to you: *What is our role in this shake up? How do we 'be' with the devastation of our life paths? Is there a way to create stability in an unstable environment?*

Nowhere to Run, Nowhere to Hide!

In any work environment, each of us brings with us a sense of un-assuredness. And, with that comes stress, worry and perhaps a less than calm and serene demeanor. We feel helpless and powerless in the face of these turbulent times. As is the case at Naomi's company, heads of institutions are shortening the sails, battening down the hatches and throwing excess baggage overboard. We wonder if today is our day to walk the plank.

So what's the solution? Well, from a bigger picture, which is what spirituality allows us to see, there is no problem. So, no solution is required. What is required, from this spiritual, bigger picture perspective, is to remember who you are in the first place. Who were you before you were a business person, a member of a cultural or religious tradition; even before you were a man or a woman? It takes a lot of sifting through the myriad identities that we've overlaid upon our essential nature. By remembering who you really are, you come to find the calm sea within. You realize that, like Shakespeare says, we are merely players on this stage we call THIS LIFE. We can leave behind our roles, identities and characters. In doing so, we come back to the "me" underneath it all.

I googled spirituality in business and found a large number of articles and blogs that share the degree to which business people engage in spiritual conversations in the workplace. I'm not making this stuff up, attempting to convince you of the

107

paradigm shift within which we are already immersed. I encourage you to see how disempowered you can believe yourself to be, or, you can cultivate awareness and awaken to how empowered you are to empower yourself and others.

Our business institutions are the spiritual centers now. It is where we practice the essential truths of our religious and spiritual traditions. It's where we practice acceptance of what we cannot change, where we cultivate the courage to change the things we can, and develop wisdom in order to know the difference. It's where we practice compassion and gratitude, for there, but for the grace of God, go I. It is where we deliver ourselves from evil, for the sake of the well-being of every being on the planet, as well as the planet herself. It's where we practice, as Mahatma Gandhi said — being the change we wish to see.

Turbulence? You bet. It gives us the opportunity to discover clarity of knowing that there is nothing to fear but fear itself. Discovering, recognizing and acknowledging this Truth is essential to the journey.

U: Ubiquitous and Universality

I love the word ubiquitous. It's got big energy. It has a quality of being that is "bigger than", more expansive, and universal in nature. It means everywhere, ever-present, all-pervading, Universal. So yes, this does describe the aspect of spirituality in business that I want to capture — that quality of presence that is always and everywhere. It is pervasive in grace and glory, and its capacity to transform business is beyond the beyond.

Look at all of the writings on leadership and business practices that intend to provide more effective, more prosperous practices for corporations, business, investors and employees. Everyone is looking for that magic pill, the big BANG that will transfigure our current circumstance to outstanding results. Anyone willing to engage the ubiquitous and the universal? Not many people are. Its takes moxie, chutzpah, courage, and the willingness to put everything on the line. You face the death of your identity, as you've known yourself to be. You are taking the leap with vision and compelling intention — there's no stopping you when you are this committed; but are you? Are you committed enough?

My client, Aaron, in Israel, is on the verge of taking the leap. He's very good at what he does as a manager in a primo corporate position. He has the wisdom to know that he could set his sights low, and settle for safety and security. He could continue to placate his manager, saying the rights things to ensure he doesn't rock the boat. However, he hasn't hired just anyone as his executive coach. He's hired me — someone who empowers clients to think and live into the context of ubiquitous universality. This means allowing a more expansive outlook to be included in his choice-making process. This notion challenges him. It's daunting to consider a paradigm shift, especially with a wife and children to support. What is at stake is the livelihood at work for himself, his direct reports, their direct reports, and those to whom he reports. Laterally, horizontally and vertically — he makes a difference.

Aaron has an opportunity to affect the lives of many people, including the well-being of his children. By taking on a more ubiquitous perspective of the reality of life in the corporate world, and on the Earth, he gains the ability to create a more expansive perspective, where the bottom line is calculated not only by the P&L statement, but by the profitability of conscious communication, sustainability of relationships, and the inclusion of more self-empowering skill development.

One particular dilemma of engaging spirituality in business is that certain principles and concepts have to be acknowledged as ubiquitous — existing and being everywhere. Perennial philosophy is a term for principles and truths that are ubiquitous, conveyed within every religious and spiritual tradition that ever existed.

Perennial philosophy asserts that there is a single divine foundation of all religious knowledge, referred to as the universal truth. Each world religion, independent of its cultural or historical context, is simply a different interpretation of this knowledge. World religions including, but not limited to, Christianity, Islam, Judaism, Hinduism, Taoism, Confucianism, Shinto, Sikhism and Buddhism, are all derived from the same universal truth. Although the sacred scriptures of these world religions are undeniably diverse and often oppose each other, each world religion has been formed to fit the social, mental and spiritual needs of their respective epoch and culture. Therefore, perennial philosophy maintains that each world religion has flourished from the foundation of the same universal truth, making these differences superficial and able to be cast aside, revealing a religion's deeper spiritual meaning. From http://en.wikipedia.org/wiki/Perennial_philosophy

According to Aldous Huxley, author of Perennial Philosophy (1945), the perennial philosophy is: The metaphysics that recognizes a divine Reality substantial to the world of things and lives and minds; the psychology that finds in the soul something similar to, or even identical with, divine Reality; the ethic that places man's final end in the knowledge of the immanent and transcendent Ground of all being; the thing is immemorial and universal. Rudiments of the perennial philosophy may be found among the traditional lore of primitive peoples in every region of the world, and in its fully developed forms it has a place in every one of the higher religions. From: http://en.wikipedia.org/wiki/Perennial_philosophy

The gist of this book on spirituality in business has been to cultivate awareness of universal challenges and dilemmas that are part of everyday human life within a work environment. The ubiquitous nature of our humanity engages each and every one of us to discover, recognize and acknowledge the universal nature of our experiences. Regardless of your position in an organization, there are certain aspects of being human that you cannot avoid: Assessments and judgments of our successes or lack thereof, fear of rejection and humiliation, conflict and emotional triggers, desires and frustrations, creative engagement with our work, fulfillment and meaning. These are just a few of the circumstances we encounter every day, which require us to transcend our normal operating procedures — our survival strategies — and reach for a way of being that serves the highest good of all, ubiquitously — everywhere, always.

This is not rocket science. This is remembering that kindness is the most powerful force of change we have. Through the practice of kindness, we transcend egoic conflict and move to a more compassionate, heart-centered engagement, which acknowledges all parties for their unique perspectives, gifts and contribution to the unfolding of Universal expansion. That is what we are all doing here — contributing to Universal expansion.

As the paradigm shifts, our acts originate effortlessly from a ground of being that is self-empowering and empowers others to live and work in right relationship with oneself, our teams, our investors — the planet and the Universe at large. It's big work, but that's why you've come at this time. You knew we'd need you and your fullest, most passionate desire to have it unfold perfectly. I'm glad you are here.

V: Vulnerability

You must have seen this coming!

From the moment we are born we are vulnerable to — well, to everything. Very quickly, and as best we can, we begin to tap into strategies that keep us invulnerable to starvation. We begin to calculate, developing strategies to get what we need and perhaps what we want. Our parents can distinguish a cry for a diaper change from one that says I'm hungry. We learn very quickly how to take care of the situation and to minimize vulnerability.

As calculating as we can be, there comes a moment when we are whacked upside the head with the proverbial 2×4, which requires an even shrewder way of being, in order to avoid further vulnerability. We continually build our arsenal of survival mechanisms until we've established a strategy that keeps us winning at getting what we want, when we want it; until it doesn't. At some point, it becomes clear that this winning strategy limits what's possible. Though you remain invulnerable, which seems like a good thing, you are unable to access what's necessary in order to have what you want. The only way to shift this process is to willingly risk being vulnerable.

Earlier I talked about that moment when you decided to be invulnerable. In that instant, what occurred to trigger that decision was too painful and too challenging for a little kid to handle. You had no one to tell you that you would be okay. In that moment you were all alone, and alone you made the choice to protect yourself at all cost.

At some point in each lifetime, we are required to revisit that moment and be willing to risk what we couldn't as a child. We have to trade invulnerability for what we want. As an adult, we've had plenty of experiences where we calculatingly traded our invulnerability for vulnerability. Trying out for various sports, asking someone for a date, applying to colleges and jobs, asking for a raise; each of these were instances where we chose vulnerability in order to get what we wanted. This is a very good thing and indicates we know how to stretch and strengthen the muscles required to take a risk. What allows us to risk some times and not others? What allows us to be more vulnerable in some circumstances while not in others?

In the world of business, most of us are limited by our winning strategies, remaining invulnerable. This keeps us safe, secure and stable but also most of the time unfulfilled. For example, my client Patricia has phenomenal skills in her line of business, but is scared to death of losing the stability she's created, even though she is terribly miserable in her work. She is not alone. Many of us feel the same way as Patricia.

When Patricia thinks about quitting her job and changing careers, she feels like a tiny incapable human being. In that moment, she's calling up the young child who is too vulnerable to step out into the big scary world. Think about it for just a moment. We approach this moment of risk as if we were that young innocent child, not the grown-up who has taken risks and succeeded.

Believe it or not, the evidence is stacked in your favor that you will survive taking risks. Yet, you hold on to that childhood instance in your life when all was lost. You were only a little kid and didn't have the maturity to deal with the fallout. You were lost and not yet found. Yes, *not yet found.*

When what's at stake is more important to you than the safety of your invulnerable prison, you have the opportunity to find yourself. Lost or left behind, you can remember and reclaim any and all aspects of the 'you' you left behind. It is an exquisite reunion, one you'll never forget.

Patricia knows that hiding within her "protective" walls will never replace the feeling of fulfillment outside. At this moment,

117

while you read this, she is calculating what's at stake and if it's worth the risk.

Our business, the work we bring to the world, is the most crucial aspect of self-expression. And self-expression, in whatever form that takes, is essential to thriving. By empowering ourselves and others to step past walls that only *seem* to keep us safe, we create an opening in the current reality for a paradigm shift. You have no idea the positive repercussion that follows such an act. Even the slightest movement in the direction of what you want, which requires courage and faith, will reward you with a sense of accomplishment that is in itself a beautiful reward. Give it a try — what have you got to lose?

W: Will

I've been thinking about this section for a while, specifically what I had in mind to communicate regarding our will. The third step of the Twelve Step Program came to mind:

We turn our will over to the care of a higher power as we understand it.

(The original version is: *We made a decision to turn our will and our lives over to the care of God, as we understand him.* Quite often, people are turned off by the religious components of the twelve steps, so I am paraphrasing in order to hopefully make this more palatable).

What I realized was, throughout our lifetimes, we've quite often turned our will over to higher powers. From the time we take our first breath we turn our will over to our doctors, parents, teachers, and coaches. We turn it over to our employers, lovers and sometimes our children. We turn it over for the purpose of physical survival as well as emotional, spiritual and economic survival. We turn our lives and our will over to those who require respect and authority over us. As a consequence, we often learn to choose disempowering interpretations about ourselves and our lives. We learn to compromise and compensate for the loss of our will, our spirit and life-force. We then choose to use our will in ways that temporarily relieve suffering of such a loss (most of this is unconscious).

In a sense, we have surrendered our essential-self, which handicaps our capability to fulfill our highest Self-expression. Instead, we compensate for what is no longer accessible by justifying our existence with what we do and what we get paid to do. Thus, connection with our life force (God as we know him) is lost, and we now use our willfulness to do what we are "supposed" to do or what is mandated to us by those we give authority to.

To be willful is to thrive and yet, to be willful as a child or as an adult is often met with punishment, rejection or humiliation. We've all learned to temper our will for the will of those of higher authority. Feelings of powerlessness to make a difference in the world turn us toward using our will to create activities that numb us. TV, food, gaming, sex, just to name a few, keep us from experiencing the desperateness that underlies apathy and dis-ease caused by surrendering our will to others. When we choose to capitulate our will, we lose connection to our essential nature and to Universal Consciousness, the source of all that is.

Not my will but Thy will be done

In the world of business, each of us is required sooner or later to discover what is ours to do. Recognizing and acknowledging this requires us to observe how we choose to use our will, and whether or not it is in service to our highest knowing. This is the moment when great leaders are born, as well as great managers and team players. When we choose to use our will to play it safe and stay small, we are willingly fencing ourselves off from what we want to avoid. That closure, however, will inevitably precipitate a breakdown. Our survival mechanisms — the way we use our willfulness to suffer, settle and survive will need an overhaul.

I have no doubt that each of us is exactly where we need to be in order to figure out what's truly ours to do. Willingly and courageously inching our way through the maze of confusion, and willfully taking a stand for a quality of being that will transform corporate culture. This is a self-transcending process for each individual and for each business institution.

We are all essentially in the process of recovery from the influences of our current paradigm: primarily, our fear-based reality. Any trauma we've experienced has to be worked through, in order to reintegrate our souls and our will back into our bodies. Business environments are a perfect environment for this healing to occur, because of the multitude of opportunities we meet daily to use our will in alignment with our highest truth. Sometimes we can do this on our own, sometimes we have to reach out for help, and sometimes we feel like we are beyond help. At that time, we realize that we've turned our will over to a "higher power" that has failed us. With no hope in sight, where do we turn?

We've corrupted our own identity by willingly surrendering our life force in the name of suffering, settling, and surviving. How do we begin to willingly choose differently, in service to the will of our own highest power — our own highest truth?

Ending corruption within ourselves and, ultimately, our organizations, is only possible when we are willing to notice that corruption is within all of us. Only through each of us can we begin to practice something different.

When I was a young man, I wanted to change the world. I found it was difficult to change the world, so I tried to change my nation.

When I found I couldn't change the nation, I began to focus on my town. I couldn't change the town and as an older man, I tried to change my family.

Now, as an old man, I realize the only thing I can change is myself, and suddenly I realize that if long ago I had changed myself, I could have made an impact on my family. My family and I could have made an impact on our town. Their impact could have changed the nation and I could indeed have changed the world. ~ Unknown Monk (around 1100 A.D.)

At what point do we consciously choose to turn our will over to an invisible source of support? Most of us wait until it is beyond obvious that our lives have become unmanageable, and we are rendered powerless over the addictive ways we chose to deal with our circumstances. At this point, too frequently, we hurt like hell and feel as if we have no other option but to turn our will and our lives over to the care of this Universal Source of all that is (God, as we understand him).

Though it is the same process as surrendering our will to mundane authority figures, consciously turning our will over to God as we understand him feels scary. Consciously choosing to surrender is different than using the usual "victim" logic and justification: *I have to because my boss says I have to; I have to if I want this promotion; I have to if I want that SOB to stop breathing down my neck.* Surrendering our will in the mundane/usual way requires a surrendering of our integrity and dignity. I think that's very telling. We can stop this corrupt practice by concealing the denial that is going on inside each of us.

Regardless of our work environment, we have the opportunity to notice how we use our will to empower or disempower ourselves by giving our power to those we choose to have authority over us. How has it served you to exercise your will in this way? What's it like for you to live with these choices? Are there other choices that would be more empowering for you and your company?

Notice when what you want isn't in your highest good or the highest good of anyone! And, continually ask yourself if what you think or do is in your highest truth and highest good. If it isn't, you might want to engage with someone who can support you in making the changes you want to ensure an extraordinarily empowering work experience.

X: Xenophobia

Xenophobia is defined at Wikipedia as "an unreasonable fear or hatred of foreigners or strangers, or of that which is foreign or strange."

My sense is that we are all xenophobic. We are all wary of new people, new things and ideas, even when such ideas are proven to improve bottom lines, in a financial sense, and/or any other aspect of life. We are often too afraid to let go of our inflexibility and invulnerability to try something new.

It's not uncommon for those who experience xenophobia to fear losing their roles, their positions, and their identity. We experience suspicion of other people's activities and become aggressive, desiring the elimination of the other's presence in order to secure for ourselves a presumed sense of stability. This behavior supports a foundation built on worry and anxiety — an unstable platform upon which to build a survival strategy. It will topple under the slightest tremor.

Even with economic and environmental instability that may bring about the extinction of our economic system, or worse yet, the extinction of our species, we are too terrified to look beyond our current context and status quo to explore those means that will create a paradigm shift into a more authentic experience of stability. Xenophobia sets off denial, among other survival strategies, as a way of avoiding what we don't want to face. It's too scary!

It doesn't even have to be about global situations. It could be about bringing more effective processes into management and leadership roles. It could be about recognizing that it's intimidating to be human in a work environment that isn't tolerant of its human resource, because we are sometimes unpredictable, uncontrollable and fallible. It could be about entering into a dialog with yourself about what you are afraid of and how you behave at work in response to that fear. Confronting these fears reveal interesting patterns of being that aren't pathological; they're just strategies we've developed in order to cope.

We are afraid of being afraid. Under the scrutiny of others, we could be revealed as weak and inadequate, that we are replaceable, or that we have no value whatsoever. We are all afraid of being found out that we are not who we pretend to be. When faced with strangers or new people, we are fearful that they may see what we've been hiding all along.

Any phobia starts with a seed of thought that we believe is real. We cannot overcome any fear until we distinguish the underlying belief. Most our fears are irrational and have no evidence to support them in the current paradigm. Most of these fears we took on in our childhood years. We never stopped to assess the degree of truth upon which they were based. Our cultures, religions and economic institutions, in general, support the fear-based reality within which we operate, and they stifle any development that will threaten their position. I believe we are encouraged to be xenophobic.

Alternatives to western medicines, fossil fuels, capitalism and fundamental religions, regardless of decades of research that point to the value they bring, are feared and perceived as serious threats to our well-being.

Within our business environments, how is xenophobia encouraged? Your institution may be a rare example of freedom from such a mechanism; however, the truth is that the underlying fear we carry is so unconscious that we remain unaware of it. Only through inquiry and direct confrontation with our dearly held beliefs are we able to discover fearful patterns of being that began as a response to a single moment in our lives.

Spirituality is a frightening concept to many. Though sought after by millions, it also scares the bejeezus out of us. We don't understand it. It makes no sense to put trust and faith in an unseen source, and yet people find comfort when engaged in practices that support spiritual development. People feel better about themselves and others. There's a calmness and peace in the environment, and people are more productive and happier when cultivating spiritual awareness. Why not consciously invite this into the workplace?

All organizational dysfunctions originate from one human being whose fear-based choices permeate throughout the whole. Fear is highly contagious. The remedy is alternative in nature, for as Einstein said, you can't solve the problem with the same thinking that created it. Fearful thinking begets fear-based solutions.

How do we 'be' with our fears in a way that allows them to be recognized for what they are? We can't overcome our fears until we discover the underlying beliefs. As long as we continue to pretend we are not afraid, we'll never stop having to pretend.

What's possible through this exploration is that we recover truths, and clarify realities. This allows us to reconsider what to believe in and act from. Without such an expedition, our business environment will have no way to recover itself. The xenophobic environment will continually fail to create and produce from a highly functional perspective. When we realize that we are all unique to each other, and that our ways of being, our ideas, and the gifts we bring to the table are reflections of a larger, more expansive source, we are then empowered to be curious, willingly mining the nuggets of gold that support true innovation. This alternative exponentially empowers the essential paradigm shift.

Y: Yin and Yang

In Asian philosophy, the concept of yin and yang is used to describe how polar opposite and seemingly contrary forces are interconnected and interdependent in the natural world. They are equal qualities that give rise to each other in turn. Opposites thus only exist in relation to each other. Many natural dualities—e.g. dark and light, feminine and masculine, low and high, cold and hot— are thought of as manifestations of yin and yang (respectively). They interact within a greater whole, as part of a dynamic system. Everything has both yin and yang aspects, as light cannot exist without darkness and vice-versa, but either of these aspects may manifest more strongly in particular objects or beings, and may ebb or flow over time.

Further, whenever one quality reaches its peak, it will naturally begin to transform into the opposite quality. For example, grain that reaches its full height in summer (fully yang) will produce seeds and die back in winter (fully yin) in an endless cycle.

Yin and yang are bound together as parts of a mutual whole (i.e. you cannot have the back of a hand without the front). A way to illustrate this idea is to consider the notion of a race with only men or only women; it would disappear in a single generation. Yet, men and women *together* create new generations that allow the race to survive. The interaction of the two gives birth to things. Yin and yang transform each other. Like an undertow in the ocean, every advance is complemented by a retreat, and every rise transforms into a fall. (From Wikipedia.)

The inception of each organization or institution arrived within a thought (Yang), which moments before was part of the vast void, or sea of unconsciousness (Yin); a place of mystery, receptiveness, openness and allowing that is essential to every aspect of life. The birth of every thought, idea, project, invention and organization is a gift from this undervalued domain.

Most Westerners believe that it is our thinking, our reaching for, our doing (Yang) that procreates and manifests — not the being (Yin). When we focus on the act of creation we may ignore this aspect of being (The Yin Factor) without which life, corporation, financial and religious institutions wouldn't exist. The womb is where inception takes place. It is where creation occurs, gestates, and forms until birth.

The decline of our world powers and many of the structures that support the notion of human domination have been built through Yang-ness: Think, build, do, grow. Ignoring the Yin Factor's vital contribution to life has created such an imbalance that the inevitable is occurring — The Fall; and we are surprised, overwhelmed and unprepared!

This isn't a bad thing. It's part of the Universal laws of change. Consider the apple tree. From winter's gift of rest comes a life force in Spring that manifests as blossoms. These over time become fruit, which fully ripen and fall to the ground. If the fruit is not eaten it will decompose and rot, nourishing the tree, while its own seeds generate new life. There's nothing bad about this cycle and we wouldn't consciously want to change a thing about it. Nevertheless, due to our one-pointed focus on production and rewards, we ignore the necessary Yin-ness of our being, and push so hard that we exhaust our resources. Just like the apple tree after creating its bounty, we too need winter to rest. We too need to focus our attention away from production and allow ourselves to be immersed in the experience of the fall. Just like the apple at the moment of full impeccability, like a fetus in the womb, or the moment before a corporation goes public, something happens (Yin-ness — the great mystery), and the fully formed organism has to detach from its source. The birthing process has completed and the fertile ground is ready to receive and engage with this new creation. Inevitably, growth, decline and death are intertwined for every single entity, thought and institution. Those focused solely on the Yang-ness of life distract and deny the essentialness of the unavoidable decline and death.

Steve Jobs, founder of Apple Computer, was a beautiful reflection of the Yin Yang principle. His words reflect the wisdom of including the intuition and the knowing that resides in the fecund void. *Have the courage to follow your heart and your intuition. They somehow already know what you truly want to become."* His brilliance wasn't born out of his intellect alone (Yang-ness), but was nurtured and nourished through his openness and receptivity to an illogical and irrational aspect of life (Yin-ness). His famous speech given at the 2005 commencement ceremonies at Stanford University encouraged listening to and embracing our own highest knowing, and acting in our own highest good; for in doing so we act in the highest good for all. Balancing our intellect with the heart and the soul — through which the Great Mystery reveals itself — we will organically fulfill our life purpose and contribute in our own unique way to the unfolding of the Universe.

We want our lives, our projects, our creations and our businesses to come to their full fruition — and we expect that they continue to sustain that level of fruition. However, we continually ignore that all things have a growth and a decline phase. It's true of universes, galaxies, stars, planets, plants, animals, humans and their creations. Engaging consciously with this reality will allow all of us to accept what we cannot change and to cultivate the courage to engage with life in the way we can. We will rest in winter's embrace, renewing ourselves while incubating unknown possibilities. Embracing our Yin-ness inevitably will contribute to the much-needed balance of yin and yang principles, as the paradigm shifts.

Z: Zenith

The Zenith is described as the highest point, or state, to have ended and thus arrived at the highest level of development. It is also considered the culmination of all that has gone before.

From a spiritualist's point of view, the zenith may be enlightenment or atonement (read as at-one-ment): As in, the Dali Lama stopped at a hotdog stand and said to the vendor, "Make me one with everything."

We've arrived at the end of this book and thus we are arriving at the Zenith, the culmination of twenty-six letters of the alphabet, and the ABC's of spirituality and business. When I began writing, I didn't see that the interweaving of concepts over time could perhaps even lead toward enlightenment. I watched as each letter and word built upon what came before. One practice led to the next. In hindsight, it all makes perfect sense.

The willingness (W) to allow and accept (A), trust (T) and practice (P); to choose (C) in service to one's highest good and highest truth, takes intention and integrity (I) to courageously face potential loneliness. Taking the leap of faith (L) all by yourself — that's the only way it can be done!

A Zenith can be that jumping off point; as for a fledgling eagle, who for the very first time steps off the edge of its nest and realizes flight. A Zenith can also be the return from a practice or journey that has brought with it insights that have been life-changing; even transformational. This leads me to a story I'd like to share:

In service to growing myself professionally (and inevitably, personally), I stepped off the edge into the spiritual abyss, never for a moment considering that the fall alone would break down every reality I ever believed to be true. I thought I was spiritually and personally evolved enough that it would be a romp in the park - not a deep purification process that macerated every limiting perception and way of being I relied upon.

Throughout this time I witnessed over and over that "I'm not that, nor that, nor that..." in relation to my identity as a woman, a highly credentialed individual, as someone who sailed across the ocean and had written two books. Over and over, I negated all of the things I had tried to be and be seen for, and all the ways I pretended to hide, in order to avoid my own fear of invisibility, vulnerability and worthlessness. Neither was I the anxiety, the anger, or sadness. I wasn't that which had given up my main source of income and continually drained my retirement savings. I wasn't any of it, and it all had to go!

Then, I participated in a shamanic journey. The vehicle for this journey was a rattle that was shaken consistently for 30 minutes. I experienced the moment of death when I realized that none of what I achieved or had tried to achieve actually mattered. As I experienced what it would be like to leave my body, it was clear I would not be taking any stuff with me — none of it. Again, the question was: *If I'm not that, then what am I?* For a very long time I listened and waited, watched and experienced … nothing.

As I experienced this nothingness I came to experience myself as the space within the rattle, nothing more. I allowed myself to merge with this reality, exploring and discovering what it was like to be without my normal identifiers or ego attachments. It was unsettling to drop everything I've ever been attached to, in service to revealing a perspective. I was like the Dali Lama's hotdog: one with everything.

Once comfortable with being the space within the rattle, I became the seeds and the rattle itself. I was in the hands of that which shakes the rattle, creating sound and vibration, ultimately creating patterns of waves and particles that make up matter — the me in physical form, my thoughts and intentions. Some trip!

Experiencing this reality has been the culmination of years of this spiritual work. It is the Zenith of self-realization and self-transcendence, and, to some degree, enlightenment. I will never forget the experience of just being the space within the rattle.

We are all this — the space, the seeds, and the rattle that when shaken creates a distinctive vibrational resonance, which manifests as the unique beings we are.

I believe that wherever we are in our professional career and development, we are each at the Zenith of our own creation — the culmination of what's come before. We've reached the pinnacle of success and fulfillment, given the circumstance and belief system within which we're currently operating. In this moment, we are at an ending and thus have arrived; perched and prepared for a new day's adventure.

Each day brings an opportunity to acknowledge the Zenith of our choice-making, a moment that reveals the manifestation of what we make important or essential. We can look around and observe how we've made a difference in the office, in our community, in the world. In this moment, we can choose how to step into the paradigm shift that we are creating. I guarantee your flight will have you soar beyond your wildest imagination.

In regard to your career, what has been your Zenith thus far? How would you define this point? What are the qualities of the

140

experience that has this be the highest level of professional development for you, as yet?

Or, your Zenith may be that moment when you realize that everything you've ever accomplished, all the money you've acquired, the promotions, the power and prestige, has no relevance to the quality of fulfillment and meaning you've experienced in your life. The culmination of everything thus far has brought you to this moment, when you decide that this is your moment to begin anew. Now, LEAP!

*****

Acknowledgements

I'd first like to acknowledge Himanshu Jhamb for inviting me to write at ActiveGarage.com. Though I've written many blogs before, writing specifically about spirituality in business was edgy for me, and I so appreciated Himanshu's expansive bandwidth to consider my work valuable to his readers.

Thirdly, I'd like to acknowledge Kim Harris who took on the job of editing these chapters after having been blogs. We both thought the task would be easy and take no time at all. Kim, however, is dedicated to perfection when it comes to the written word, and she went through each chapter with a fine tooth comb. I so appreciated her commitment to detail. Plus, she is really fun to work with.

I have to acknowledge Google Search Engine and Wikipedia. It made researching for this book so effortless. Thank you to all of those who've created such incredible technology and to all who contributed the information and resources. We live in amazing times!

Lastly, I do not write alone. I count on the unseens of this world to bring me ideas and help sculpture them in to thoughts worthy of thinking and contemplating — perhaps even acting upon. I look to my guides and angels to ensure that every thought is complete and in alignment with the highest truth and the highest good of all who read my writing.

BIO

Dr. Rosie Kuhn is the founder of the Paradigm Shifts Coaching Group, and is a preeminent thought leader in the field of transformational coaching, coach training, and leadership development. She is the author of *Self-Empowerment 101* and *The Unholy Path of a Reluctant Adventurer, and Dilemmas of Being in Business*. She is an international keynote speaker and transformational coach to individuals, organizations, and executives world-wide.

Find out more at http://www.theparadigmshifts.com and http://www.Dr-Rosie.com. Follow her on Twitter @RosieKuhn and on Facebook: https://www.facebook.com/DrRosieKuhnAsTheParadigmShifts

www.ingramcontent.com/pod-product-compliance
Lightning Source LLC
LaVergne TN
LVHW051348080426
835509LV00020BA/3339